After the Death
of Your Spouse

Next Financial Steps for Surviving Spouses

After the Death of Your Spouse

Next Financial Steps for Surviving Spouses

Mike Piper, CPA

Dedication

As always, for you, the reader.

And for Kalinda, hopefully not any time soon.

Disclaimer

This book is not intended to be a substitute for personalized advice from a professional financial planner. Nothing contained within this text should be construed as legal or financial advice. The publisher and author make no representation or warranty as to this book's adequacy or appropriateness for any purpose. Similarly, no representation or warranty is made as to the accuracy of the material in this book.

Purchasing this book does not create any client relationship or other advisory, fiduciary, or professional services relationship with the publisher or with the author. *You alone* bear the *sole* responsibility of assessing the merits and risks associated with any financial decisions you make. And it should always be kept in mind that any investment can result in partial or complete loss.

Your Feedback Is Appreciated!

As the author of this book, I'm very interested to hear your thoughts. If you find the book helpful, please let me know! Alternatively, if you have any suggestions of ways to make the book better, I'm eager to hear that, too.

Finally, if you're dissatisfied with your purchase for any reason, let me know, and I'll be happy to provide you with a refund of the current list price of the book (limited to one refund per household).

You can reach me at: mike@simplesubjects.com.

Best Regards,
Mike Piper, CPA

Table of Contents

Immediate and Intermediate Next Steps

We're here to talk about the financial to-do items and planning considerations that crop up as a result of the death of your spouse. That's why you bought this book. And as a CPA, the money stuff is really all I'm qualified to speak to. But before we dive into all of that, let me first just say that I'm sorry you need this book. I'm sorry for your loss.

I would encourage you to be particularly forgiving with yourself during the weeks, months, and even years after your spouse's death. And please, at least consider meeting with a mental health professional. Doing so is not an admission of weakness or an admission that anything is "wrong" with you. Even in the easy stages of life, countless people (myself included) have found counseling to provide significant benefits.

1

Lots to Do, Not All of It Urgent

This book is, at its core, a to-do list. To come right out and say it: there are a lot of items you're going to have to take care of over the coming months. Fortunately, you don't have to do them all immediately. That is, some of these to-do items are *important* but not *urgent.*

And in fact, for some of these items, it's *best* if you wait. Many surviving spouses report experiencing a sort of "brain fog" in the weeks or months following their spouse's death. They find that they have difficulty concentrating and difficulty performing tasks that would normally be easy. Major, irrevocable decisions are best put off until this period is over, in cases in which it's practical to do so.

That's why this book is broken down into two parts: immediate next steps and intermediate next steps. It's difficult to put precise timeframes on these categories, because it will vary from one person to another. For instance, if your spouse was always the one to handle financial matters, then these steps will probably take you somewhat longer than they would for a surviving spouse who has always filled the role of household accountant. In addition, some people will *need* to move through these steps more quickly than other people because the death of their spouse has left them in more severe financial circumstances.

Throughout the book I have also made note of many of the to-do items that would be required of the party serving as executor, because surviving spouses are often named as the executor of their deceased spouse's estate.

Let's Keep This Brief

To be clear, the goal of this book is a modest one: to introduce you to the most critical financial tasks you'll have to accomplish during this next phase of your life. The goal is *not* to turn you into an expert on each of the topics discussed.

Also, the situation of one surviving spouse is very different from another. You may be age 29, with two young children, trying frantically to figure out how to make things work. Or maybe you're well into your retirement years, with considerable financial assets. And many of the topics discussed here deal with state law, so they'll be somewhat different for one person than for another person. Point being, there's no way to cover every single thing that every reader will have to do. And, on the flip side, some of the things discussed in this book may not apply to you.

You Can Do This, And It's Okay to Ask for Help

The amount of work may feel overwhelming at first, but you will get through it. And it's okay to hire professional help (such as an attorney, tax professional, or financial planner). Chapter 13 provides some guidance on selecting such professionals, if you decide to go that route.

You may also find that family members are willing to provide assistance. If you accept help from family or other loved ones though, be sure to keep track of who is doing what. And it's important to understand that if you are legally responsible for doing something, asking somebody else to do it doesn't relieve you of that responsibility (and may in fact be a breach of that responsibility, if the person you ask is not suited to the job). Still, even with those caveats in mind, help from loved ones can be very valuable.

While having loved ones available to help check off various to-do items can be helpful, likely the most helpful role that somebody can play is to be your trusted sounding board. You're going to have to make an assortment of decisions throughout this process, and it's likely that many of them will be in areas in which you have little or no prior experience. Having somebody you trust—and who has no financial stake in the decision—available to serve as a sanity check can be very valuable.

PART ONE

Immediate Next Steps

CHAPTER ONE

Learn the Terms
(The Estate Administration Process)

Before we go any further, it will be helpful to make sure that you have a clear understanding of many of the common terms.

First: what exactly *is* an estate? An **estate** is a legal entity that is automatically created when a person dies. The estate includes all assets and liabilities in which the decedent had an interest at his or her death. The estate exists until all the assets have been distributed to heirs or other beneficiaries. (Depending on state law, the estate must also remain open for a prescribed minimum period of time.)

The **executor** is the person named in the will to administer the estate (i.e., to gather the estate's assets, pay its debts and expenses, and distribute the remaining assets to beneficiaries). If your spouse did not have a will, if no executor is named in the will, or if the named party refuses to serve as executor, the court will appoint an **administrator** to perform the same functions. The person administering the estate (whether an executor named in the will or an administrator appointed by a court) is often referred to as the **personal representative** of the estate.

Probate is the legal process of administering an estate. Because probate functions based on state law, the specifics will vary somewhat from state to state. But in general, the process consists of filing court papers including the deceased party's will with the appropriate state/county clerk, notifying creditors that the estate is in probate, gathering the estate's assets, distributing those assets to the appropriate parties, and ultimately closing the estate.

Types of Joint Ownership

Most married people own various property jointly with their spouse. There are a few different ways in which property can be jointly owned, though, and it's important to understand the differences.

Tenancy in common is a form of joint ownership in which, when one of the owners dies, his or her share of the property passes according to his or her will.

EXAMPLE: Alfred, Bruce, and Charlie jointly own a piece of real estate as tenants in common, with each owning a 1/3 share. Charlie's will names his

7

son and daughter to equally inherit his share of the property. After Charlie's death, Alfred and Bruce will still each own a 1/3 share, and Charlie's two kids will each own a 1/6 share.

If property is owned via **joint tenancy** (alternatively referred to as **joint tenants with rights of survivorship**), when one owner dies, his or her share of the property is automatically passed to the surviving owner(s). Joint tenancy is the most common form of joint ownership between spouses.

EXAMPLE: Amanda and Barry each own a 1/2 share of a piece of real estate as joint tenants with rights of survivorship. If Barry dies, his 1/2 share will pass automatically to Amanda, leaving her as the sole owner of the property.

Note that it wouldn't make any difference if Barry's will stated that he leaves his portion of the property to his best friend Steve. Because the property is owned as joint tenants with rights of survivorship, Barry's share automatically goes to the surviving owner.

Tenancy by the entirety is a type of joint ownership that is available to married couples in some states. As with joint tenancy, when one of the two owners dies, property owned as tenants by the entirety will pass automatically to the surviving owner (in this case, the surviving spouse).

Certain states (Arizona, California, Idaho, Louisiana, Nevada, New Mexico, Texas, Washington, and Wisconsin) are known as **community property** states. In community property states, most property that a married couple comes to own during their marriage will be considered community property. Each spouse is considered to own 50% of the community property. Upon the death of one spouse, that spouse's share of the community property usually passes to the surviving spouse, unless the will states something to the contrary. Some states have an expedited probate process for such property.

What Has to Go Through Probate?

Broadly speaking, any asset owned by the deceased person must go through probate, unless it falls into one of three categories:

1. Assets that pass outside of the will to a named beneficiary. Common examples of assets in this category include IRAs, 401(k) or other employer-sponsored retirement accounts, health savings accounts (HSAs), life insurance proceeds, bank or brokerage accounts with a **transfer-on-death** or **payable-on-death** designation, or vehicles titled with a transfer on death beneficiary.

2. Property owned jointly with somebody else, in a manner that results in the surviving owner automatically inheriting the asset. Property owned as tenants by the entirety or joint tenants with rights of survivorship passes in this manner.
3. Property held in trust. Such property avoids probate because the terms of the trust govern how the assets are transferred. Note, however, that if the trust is *created* via the will (i.e., it's a **testamentary trust**) property that will be added to that testamentary trust *does* have to go through probate, because it's probating the will that creates the trust in the first place. (If you are the beneficiary or trustee of a trust, please be sure to read Appendix C: Dealing with Trusts.)

The details vary by state, but many states have separate "formal" and "informal" probate procedures. The general idea is that formal probate is for cases in which there may be disputes that need to be resolved by the court. Formal probate generally involves a hearing before a judge as well as ongoing supervision by the court. In contrast, informal probate is primarily a paperwork-only process in which the appropriate documents are simply filed with the court or other appropriate entity.

Probate for a straightforward estate typically lasts 6-12 months. In some cases though, probate can last for years, especially if there are disputes among heirs or creditors.

Depending on the size of the estate, you may be able to take advantage of a simplified "small estate" probate process. The applicable dollar limit varies from state to state though, as do the rules for which assets are counted toward that limit. (In many states, assets in the three categories above that pass outside of probate do not count toward the limit.) In addition, the *process* for handling a small estate varies from state to state. So be sure to check into the details for your state.

If the estate is small enough, you may be able to avoid probate entirely and claim the applicable assets via an affidavit (a written, sworn statement). Again, the details vary by state as far the threshold and as far as which assets are counted.

Chapter 1 Simple Summary

- An estate is a legal entity that is automatically created when a person dies. Its purpose is to gather the decedent's assets, pay his/her debts, and distribute any remaining assets to the appropriate beneficiaries.

- The personal representative (executor or administrator) is the person whose job it is to administer the estate.

- Probate is the legal process of administering the probate assets of an estate.

- Assets titled with a named beneficiary (e.g., IRAs or life insurance), with rights of survivorship (e.g., joint tenants with rights of survivorship or tenants by the entirety), or to a trust will pass to the applicable beneficiaries without having to go through probate. Most other assets will have to go through probate.

CHAPTER TWO

Getting Organized

The first order of business is to get organized. There are lots of items to take care of (many
of which have multiple steps themselves), and you
don't want anything to slip through the cracks. This
is a stressful time, and good organization is one way
to make it a little bit less stressful.

It will be helpful to create a filing system for
any physical paper records as well as a matching
system of folders on your computer. These will be
used for saving documents (e.g., bank statements)
together in the same place with related correspondence or other notes you have taken. Your circumstances will determine which folders you need, but
the following list may be a good start:

- Bank accounts (checking/savings)
- Borrowing accounts (mortgage, credit cards)
- Retirement accounts (IRA, 401(k), etc.)
- Other brokerage accounts

- Pension
- Social Security
- Insurance
- Will
- Trust
- Birth certificate, marriage certificate, death certificate (as well as any divorce-related documents from a prior marriage)
- Federal income tax
- State income tax
- Other tax documents
- Home
- Other real property (e.g., vacation or rental)
- Vehicle

Getting Copies of the Death Certificate

After getting organized, you'll have to get your hands on a number of important documents. First: certified copies of the death certificate.

The funeral home, cremation organization, or other entity handling your spouse's remains is generally required to prepare the death certificate and file it with the appropriate vital records office. They should contact you to collect the necessary information (e.g., your spouse's parents' names). Be sure to carefully check the information they have and any information you give them, because it can be a hassle to have changes made later. During that conversation, they will often ask how many copies of the death certificate you want.

Alternatively, you can get certified copies of the death certificate from the county records office or comparable entity where you live. A Google search for your city name and "death certificate" will usually get you to the right place. (You can also request death certificates from the state, but that often takes longer.) You will have to fill out a form and (usually) pay a modest fee.

You will have to decide how many copies to request, as there is a cost per copy. The number necessary will depend on how many accounts your spouse had at various places, as well as the policies of those institutions. (Some institutions will want to keep a certified copy for their own records, while others will just want to see it so that they can make a copy and return the original to you.) If you have no idea, guess on the high side (e.g., 20-30), unless the cost per copy is significant and it's critical that you minimize costs.

If your spouse was a veteran, depending on state law you may be entitled to free certified copies of the death certificate.

Depending on location, it may take up to a few weeks for the applicable government office to send you the certified copies of the death certificate.

Look for a Will

Another matter of high priority is to find your spouse's will, unless you are very confident that he or she did not have one. If your spouse had an attorney, call them. If you don't know of any attorney relationship, call the accountant, if you know of one. If that doesn't turn anything up, do a thorough search on your spouse's computer (including in their email), as well as in any filing cabinets, desk drawers, stacks of papers, and so on. If your spouse had a safe deposit box, check there as well.

If you still haven't found the will, try asking other family members or any of your spouse's close friends. It's possible that your spouse mentioned to one of them where he/she kept the will.

After all of the above, if you still can't find a will but you are confident that your spouse had one, it's probably a good idea to engage an attorney to ask how to proceed.

While you're looking for the will, you're likely to encounter a bunch of other important documents. When you find such things, file them according to the system you created. Taking a moment to do that now with each document will save you a lot of time later. (Otherwise, you're going to have to repeat this thorough search process later for each important document you need to track down.)

After you find the will, scan it, and put it in the appropriate spot in your filing system. It's not unreasonable to keep the original hardcopy in a locked location. If you find multiple wills, scan and keep all of them—and then contact an attorney.

If you do locate a will, you will be required by state law to file it with the probate court where your spouse resided at the time of death. (Depending on state law, there may be a deadline by which you have to file the will.)

Other Documents to Track Down

After you have located the will (or determined that there isn't one), the next task is to track down an assortment of other documents, and file them appropriately so that you can have quick access when needed. Some of the major documents you will want to find include the following, if applicable. (You will notice that these closely coincide with the filing system you created.)

- Bank statements, brokerage statements, and retirement account statements
- Mortgage statements and credit card statements
- Checkbook or other personal checking account ledger
- Pension records
- Social Security records

- Birth certificate, marriage certificate, change of name certificate, and any divorce-related documents from a prior marriage
- Tax returns
- Insurance policy statements and the policies themselves (including annuities as well as other types of insurance)
- Trust documents
- Vehicle title and registration
- Deeds to any real property

Take Notes!

Many people report experiencing an unusually high frequency of memory lapses during the weeks after the death of their spouse. And during this time you'll be juggling a bunch of similar multi-step processes with various bureaucracies. It's too easy to get the status of one process mixed up with another (e.g., "was it Fidelity that needed that other piece of documentation, or was that Bank of America?"). Point being, this is not the time to rely solely on memory. Take dated, detailed notes of all of your phone or in-person conversations, and save copies of all of your correspondence. (For email this happens automatically of course. But for anything sent as physical mail—or anything sent via a "contact" form on a website—keep a dated copy for yourself as well.)

For any in-person appointments, you may want to bring somebody along with you (e.g., one of your adult children), if any appropriate such parties exist and are willing. Having another person to help take notes and ask questions can be very helpful.

Chapter 2 Simple Summary

• Create a filing system so you can have quick and easy access to important documents.

• Request certified copies of the death certificate from the funeral home/cremation organization or from your county records office (or comparable entity).

• Look everywhere you can think of to find your spouse's will, unless you are very confident that no will exists. If you do find a will, scan it and keep that electronic copy in your filing system. You will need to file the original will with the probate court where your spouse was living at the time of death.

• Track down and file other important documents such as bank statements, retirement account statements, insurance policies, and tax returns.

• Take notes throughout this process. For any physical correspondence, keep a copy for yourself. For any phone conversations, take detailed dated notes. It's more work right now, but it will save you time (and stress!) in the long run.

CHAPTER THREE

Notifying
Necessary Parties

The next item of business is to get in touch with other various parties to notify them of your spouse's passing. Some of these entities will accept a simple email, while others will require various types of documentation (typically, a copy or certified copy of the death certificate, as well as one or more of their own forms). In some cases that paperwork may have to be notarized.

Some financial institutions may even require that you get a "signature guarantee" (a.k.a. medallion signature guarantee) for the paperwork. If you need such a guarantee, the easiest way to get it is generally to visit a local branch of a bank where you are a customer, with your (unsigned) paperwork in hand so that they can watch you sign it. You'll likely want to call in advance though, to check that they have somebody at the branch at that moment who is authorized to provide such a guarantee. If you are not a customer of any local banks, call around to the banks in your area to see if one can provide such a guarantee for a fee.

Again, take notes so that you know where in the process you are with each entity. And before sending any paperwork off in the mail (or handing it over to somebody in person) be sure to save a copy for your own records! If somebody insists on seeing the original copy of any document, if at all possible, insist that they make a copy and give you the original back, while you're still standing there. Don't trust that they will mail it back to you on some later date.

Cancel Upcoming Appointments

A good first step is to look at your spouse's calendar. If you see any upcoming appointments (e.g., doctor or dentist visits), call to cancel those. Not only is this a courteous thing to do, it could save you some money.

Contact Your Spouse's Employer

If your spouse was still employed at the time of his or her death, the employer will likely owe the estate for unpaid wages and unused vacation time. Contact the employer to make sure that this money is paid to the estate. As we'll discuss in the next chapter, the personal representative should open a bank account for the estate. These amounts for unpaid wages and unused vacation should be paid into that account.

At the same time, inquire with the employer as to whether they provided any life insurance coverage.

Finally, inquire as to whether there is a health savings account (HSA) or flexible spending account (FSA) with a balance. FSA balances are "use it or lose it"—any amounts not spent at the end of the plan year are generally forfeited. So be sure to promptly request reimbursement from the FSA for any qualifying medical expenses that occurred up to the date of your spouse's death.

If you inherit a health savings account (HSA) from your spouse, it becomes an HSA in your name, as if it had been your account all along. If anybody inherits the account from you though (anybody other than a new spouse, that is), the entirety of the funds will be automatically distributed and taxable to the beneficiary. In contrast, if you spend the HSA assets on qualified medical expenses, the distributions are tax-free. Point being, you usually want to spend these balances down, to the extent that you have qualified medical expenses, in order to take advantage of tax-free distributions.

Collecting Life Insurance and Other Death Benefits

If your spouse had life insurance coverage, you will have to notify the insurance company of your spouse's death so that the beneficiary (likely you) can receive the death benefits to which they are entitled.

Some people have multiple insurance policies. Just because you have found one doesn't mean that that's the only one. Be sure to check for others. And as noted above, be sure to check with your spouse's employer as to whether there's any life insurance coverage through them.

Finally, some annuities provide death benefits to named beneficiaries. So if your spouse owned an annuity, you will want to notify that insurance company as well. (If your spouse owned an annuity which had already begun making payments, the insurance company will need to be notified in order to adjust the payment as necessary.)

It can be helpful here to go through old bank records, including checks. There may be one or more policies you don't know about, and identifying amounts paid to insurance companies can be the critical step to identifying such a policy.

If you and your spouse have worked with a financial advisor, insurance agent, tax professional, or attorney, ask them. They might know about a policy that you don't know about.

There's also a "Life Insurance Policy Locator Service" website offered by the National Association of Insurance Commissioners. After you submit an online form, the service will ask participating companies to search their records for a life insurance policy or annuity contract in the name of the deceased that you entered.

If you are the beneficiary of a life insurance policy, you will often be given multiple choices for how to receive the proceeds (e.g., as a lump sum or as a stream of payments over a particular period of time). Working with a financial planner may be useful here. (See Chapter 13 for a discussion of finding a financial planner.)[1]

Also of note: if your spouse died via accidental death, it's possible that any life insurance policies he/she had will provide an amount beyond just the normal stated death benefit. Be sure to check the policy. Some credit cards also provide a death benefit if accidental death occurs while traveling on a trip paid for with the card in question.

When going through this process, if an insurance company asks for the policy itself (whether life insurance or annuity), be sure to scan it or make

---

[1] One concern that many surviving spouses have is that taking the proceeds as a lump sum (i.e., in one year) will result in a large tax bill. Life insurance death benefits are not taxable as income though. So at least from a tax point of view, there's no downside to taking the lump-sum option with a life insurance death benefit.

a copy before sending it in. You absolutely want to have your own record of the policy details.

Worker's Compensation

If your spouse died at work or as a result of a work-place-related injury or illness, you may qualify for worker's compensation survivor benefits. Search your state's department of labor website for more information. Consulting with an attorney with expertise in this area is also likely to be helpful.

Health and Dental Insurance

You will want to notify your health and dental insurance providers promptly, in order to adjust your coverage. For example, if it was just you and your spouse—no kids in the household—there's no sense in paying for two-person coverage anymore.

If you were covered under your spouse's employment, obtaining new coverage is a *very* high priority. Step #1: check with human resources at your spouse's employer to find out exactly when your coverage will terminate. (Some employers, especially those with strong unions, continue coverage for a significant period after the death.)

You can choose to extend coverage through your spouse's employer for up to 36 months under COBRA. Coverage through COBRA will probably be considerably more expensive though, because you will have to pay the full premium (plus a 2% administrative fee) going forward, as opposed to having the policy subsidized by the employer.

If you are employed in a position that offers health insurance, coverage through your employer may be your most affordable option. (Loss of coverage due to the death of your spouse is a qualifying event to enroll in coverage outside of open enrollment season.)

Another option is to purchase coverage through the Affordable Care Act exchange. While you can normally only enroll during the annual Open Enrollment Period, you qualify for a Special Enrollment Period that lasts for 60 days from the date on which coverage provided by your spouse's employer is terminated. (Please note though that if you enroll for coverage via COBRA, you will be locked out of Affordable Care Act coverage until the next Open Enrollment Period.)

Finally, if you have children under age 19, they may qualify for coverage under Medicaid or Children's Health Insurance Program (CHIP). There are income limits, which vary by state, but if your household will have less income going forward due to your spouse's death, your children may now qualify whereas they would not have previously. If your children do qualify, the best option may be to purchase coverage for yourself via your employer, COBRA, or the Affordable Care Act, while getting CHIP coverage for your children.

This is obviously a lot of options to consider. But it's important to think it through, both because coverage can be expensive and because a gap in coverage can be disastrous. There may be one or more non-profit organizations in your area that can guide you through such decisions.

Homeowner's or Renter's Insurance

For your homeowner's or renter's insurance policy, it's likely that the policy won't need to be modified, but it's prudent to get in touch with the insurer just to check.

Ongoing Vehicle Costs

Your spouse's car insurance provider should also be notified, so that the policy can be canceled or so that they can be removed from the policy. (Note that if you plan to drive the vehicle, you will need to make sure that you are still insured as a driver of the vehicle.)

If your spouse was leasing a car, you may have an option to cancel that lease, though there will probably be an early termination fee.

If your spouse owned a car that you will not need, you'll probably want to sell it—and the sooner the better, not just to free up the cash but also so that you don't have to pay car insurance and (if applicable) property tax any longer than necessary. Once you do sell the car, cancel the insurance and ask the insurance company for a refund for any unused months (e.g., if the premium is paid on an annual basis).

Social Security Administration

We'll discuss details of the Social Security benefits available to surviving spouses later, in Chapter 6. But for now, know that you will need to contact the Social Security Administration in order to claim at least one sort of benefit. In addition, if your spouse was receiving Social Security benefits, it's important for the SSA to know to turn that benefit off. The payment for the month of death will have to be returned, regardless of the day of the month on which your spouse died. (For example, if your spouse died in February, the deposit for February, which is paid in March, would have to be returned.) If the SSA is not notified and they continue to pay, you'll be required to pay the money back later anyway. And that just creates even more hassle, which you do not need right now.

Please be forewarned though that if the bank account into which the SSA was making deposits was solely in your spouse's name, the SSA will inform that bank of the death (in order to reclaim the necessary amount) and the bank will likely freeze the account. The account will remain frozen until the bank is provided with the proper documentation that somebody has been appointed as the personal representative of the estate.

Banks & Other Financial Institutions

Once you have received copies of the death certificate, any financial institution with which your spouse had a relationship should be notified. This includes places where your spouse owned an account as a joint owner.

With each account, take careful note of how it is titled, including whether there is anybody listed as a payable-on-death or transfer-on-death beneficiary.

Similarly, for retirement accounts such as IRAs, 401(k) accounts, or 403(b) accounts, inform the financial institution of your spouse's death and ask about the beneficiary designations on the account. (We'll talk about your options for any inherited accounts later, in Chapter 8.)

For property that passes automatically to another party (including retirement accounts with a designated beneficiary, non-retirement accounts with a designated transfer-on-death or payable-on-death beneficiary, or accounts owned as joint tenants with rights of survivorship or tenants by the entirety) notifying the financial institution of your spouse's death should begin that transfer process.

If your spouse had a defined benefit pension, you'll need to inform the provider, so that they can end or adjust the payment as necessary.

You'll also want to close any of your spouse's credit card accounts and cancel any debit cards. But before doing so, be sure to change over any auto-pay subscriptions that you want to maintain that were being charged to that card. If it is a joint credit card account, rather than canceling it, ask to have it changed to be in just your name. (If there's any remaining balance, you can ask them to cancel it or reduce it. Sometimes they do, and there's no harm in asking.)

Some surviving spouses worry that if they inform the mortgage lender that their spouse has died, the loan will immediately come due. Do not worry. Federal law prohibits a lender from activating "due-on-sale" provisions when a home passes from the borrower to any relative (including a spouse) as a result of the borrower's death.

Educational Institutions

If you have a child (or children) currently in college, it's a good idea to get in touch with the school's financial aid office. If your spouse's death has significantly reduced your household income, there may be additional resources that are now available to you.

While less likely, the same goes for private high schools and grade schools—they may have the ability to provide some tuition assistance.

Other Ongoing Costs

It's worth taking the time to identify any ongoing subscriptions that you have, to see whether they should be canceled (e.g., a TV streaming service that only your spouse used) or adjusted (e.g., your phone plan). Going through your recent credit card and bank statements can help identify any such recurring expenses.

Before cancelling your spouse's phone service though (or getting rid of his/her phone), be sure to save any data (e.g., photos, contact information, texts, saved voicemails) that you will want to access later.

Utility Companies

If the utility bills are solely in your spouse's name, if you keep paying the bills, the utility companies will continue to provide service and probably won't care. However, it's a good idea to contact the utility companies to have the accounts changed to your name. If your name is not on the account, you won't be able to make any changes to the service. In addition, after you eventually pass away, the personal representative of *your* estate will have more of a mess to deal with if your spouse's name is still the only name on the account (because adjusting services will require them to provide documentation of your spouse's death, which may be more difficult to find at that point).

Transferring Title of Other Property

You'll also need to notify any other necessary parties so that property owned by your spouse can have title transferred appropriately. Since financial accounts have already been covered by this point, this primarily leaves vehicles and real estate.

For vehicles, the entity to notify would be the local DMV. A relevant point here is that some states actually allow for title of a vehicle that was owned solely by the deceased spouse to transfer to a surviving spouse without having to go through probate, if there was no other party named as a transfer-on-death beneficiary on the title and the deceased's will does not state otherwise.

For real estate, the entity to notify could be known as the Recorder of Deeds, Land Records Office, County Registrar, or something similar. They will generally need a certified copy of the death certificate and potentially a signed affidavit (which might need to be notarized) or a court order. Depending on how the property was owned (e.g., your spouse was the sole owner or he/she owned it jointly with you via one of the forms of joint owner-ship discussed in Chapter 1) as well as the law in the place where the property is located, a new deed may be necessary.

If your spouse owned real property in another state, an "ancillary probate" process in that state may even be required.

Other Parties to Notify

Finally, there are several other entities that should be informed, so that they can update their records. This is important because it reduces the likelihood of post-mortem identity theft. Yes, post-mortem identity theft really *does* happen. It's attractive to thieves because it's more likely to go undetected. And it's a giant hassle to the surviving spouse, even though you should ultimately not be held responsible for any fraudulent charges/debts.

The list of organizations to inform of your spouse's death would include at least:

- All three credit reporting agencies (Equifax, Experian, and TransUnion);
- Your local DMV;
- The IRS, if they have not already been notified;
- The State Department, if your spouse had a passport;

- Any other government entity that had any relationship with your spouse (e.g., Department of Veterans Affairs); and
- Any healthcare providers that have not yet been notified.

Chapter 3 Simple Summary

- Notify any insurance company where your spouse had life insurance or any other policy with a death benefit.

- Contact your spouse's employer to have any unpaid wages paid to the estate. Also ask about life insurance and HSA/FSA balances.

- Update your health and car insurance policies as necessary. Reassess other ongoing costs (e.g., subscriptions, phone plan) to see what should be updated or canceled.

- Notify any financial institutions with which your spouse had a relationship. Ask about beneficiary designations on each account.

- Notify all three credit reporting agencies, to minimize the risk of identity theft.

- Notify the DMV and county records office so title can be transferred appropriately for any vehicles or real estate your spouse owned (including jointly).

- Notify the SSA, the IRS, and any other government agency that had any relationship with your spouse.

CHAPTER FOUR

Initial Responsibilities as Personal Representative

Through this chapter I am assuming that you are the personal representative (or one of multiple personal representatives) of your spouse's estate. If you are not, then these responsibilities will fall to somebody else. But even in that case, you'll want to stay informed as to how the process is coming along, as your interests are certainly affected.

As the personal representative (PR) you are responsible for gathering the deceased's assets and distributing them to the appropriate parties. You are allowed to hire professional assistance (e.g., an attorney) with this, and it may be wise to do so, especially if there are anticipated disagreements among the beneficiaries, if any of the terms of the will are ambiguous, or if the estate's debts exceed its assets.

Your local probate court may also offer some degree of guidance with the process—online FAQ pages, guides, necessary forms available online, etc.

The details vary from state to state and even from county to county. This chapter (and Chapter 7 for later steps) attempts to provide a general guideline, in roughly the order the events would occur.

Apply to Be Appointed as Personal Representative

If you are named in the will as PR (and you do in fact want to serve as PR) you will have to apply with the court to officially be appointed as such. Similarly, if there was no will and you want to serve as PR, you'll have to ask the court to appoint you as PR.

If you are approved as the PR, the court will issue you a document or series of documents (often referred to as **letters testamentary**, **letters of authority**, or something similar) authorizing you to act on behalf of the estate.

Personal Representative Compensation

The PR is entitled to reasonable compensation for his or her efforts. The will might dictate the amount of compensation, or it may be determined by state law. The PR has the option to decline compensation, and if you will be receiving the entire estate, it likely makes sense to do so, given that such compensation is taxable as income.

Proving the Will's Validity

Just because a will exists doesn't necessarily mean that it is legally valid. Many states provide that self-proving wills are presumptively valid. **Self-proving wills** are those signed by the testator, witnessed by two or more individuals who certify that the will was signed by the decedent or testator, where all signatures are notarized.

If somebody objects to the will's validity, the court will have a hearing and make a ruling on the matter. If somebody does make such an objection, be sure to wait until the court has officially determined that the will is valid before relying on it.

Fiduciary Duty

As personal representative you have a **fiduciary duty** to the estate and its beneficiaries and creditors. This means that, in all of your actions as PR, you must put the interests of the estate and its beneficiaries/creditors above your own interests (other than to the extent that you are one of the beneficiaries).

Your fiduciary duty also includes an obligation to take prudent care of the assets. For example, if you invest the assets in a risky way, beneficiaries of the estate could sue you for any losses.

You also have an obligation to use the estate's assets to pay any valid debts of your deceased spouse and to distribute assets to the appropriate heirs. But don't go doing that just yet! For reasons discussed later in this chapter, it is generally prudent to make a full inventory of the estate's assets and liabilities before distributing any assets. (Paying creditors and distributing assets will be discussed later, in Chapter 7.)

Finally, never lend yourself money from the estate or sell yourself something from the estate without explicit permission from the probate court. Both could be seen as violations of your fiduciary duty.

Notify Other Parties

The probate court will likely require you as PR to mail a notification of the probate process to anybody who might inherit (i.e., beneficiaries or heirs).

In addition, if you are aware that your spouse owed money to any parties ("creditors"), you must notify those creditors of your spouse's death and the probate proceedings. You may also be required to publish a legal notice in a local newspaper, in order to alert any other creditors or other parties who might have a claim against the estate.

Get a Bank Account and Taxpayer ID for the Estate

In order to keep the estate's assets separate from your own and to facilitate recordkeeping, you will probably need to set up a bank account in the name of the estate. Any assets in bank accounts that were owned solely by your spouse and which do not have payable-on-death or transfer-on-death beneficiary designations should be transferred into this new account. Any income, such as wages not yet paid, should be paid into this account as well. This is also the account from which any creditors will be paid.

This bank account will also be used to pay the estate's expenses (e.g., hiring an appraiser for certain property).

In order to set up that bank account, you will need letters testamentary from the probate court and a taxpayer ID for the estate. For the taxpayer ID, search for "EIN application" on IRS.gov. (A taxpayer ID is also referred to as an "employer identification number" or EIN because in most cases the entity applying for an ID is a business.) An important thing to note here is that it is *free* to get an EIN on IRS.gov. There are other websites that will charge you to fill out this application on your behalf, but there's absolutely no need to pay for it.

You will also need to file Form 56 with the IRS to notify them that you are the personal representative of the estate.

Take an Inventory

Next, the PR must take a formal inventory of the estate's assets and liabilities (debts).

For each asset, list what it is and its current value (if easily determinable). Also list how the asset was owned (i.e., whether it was owned solely by your deceased spouse or owned jointly with you or another party). If the property was owned jointly, it's important to know what type of joint ownership was involved (e.g., tenancy in common, joint tenancy with rights of survivorship, etc.). Also be sure to note if any property has a payable-on-death or transfer-on-death designation. Right now, the goal is to include everything—even assets that will pass directly to a named beneficiary without probate (e.g., an IRA).

For things that do not have significant financial value and which are unlikely to be of significant sentimental value to anybody, you can group them into a category (e.g., "clothing" as opposed to individually listing each t-shirt).

Hopefully you already have a good sense of what financial assets your spouse owned. But it's important to check for other assets and accounts—many people have been surprised by assets they didn't know about! Looking for account statements in the mail (or email) is a good first step. It's also important to check through your spouse's physical files if they kept any, as well as looking through files on your spouse's computer(s) to see if you can find any financial documents.

Contacting your spouse's prior employers is a good idea, to inquire whether there are any 401(k) or similar accounts that haven't been rolled over.

Another good way to track down other accounts is to look at prior year's tax returns. Form 8949 lists assets sold in a given year, which can help to alert you to brokerage accounts you may not have known about. Schedule B of Form 1040 lists interest and dividends received, which can also direct you toward accounts owned by your spouse. Also look for any of the various versions of Form 1099 (e.g., Form 1099-INT, Form 1099-DIV, or Form 1099-R) as they can inform you about accounts as well. In short, you want to be able to go through the Form 1040 and state "yes, I know what this income is from" for every line item of income. If there's any income that you don't know where it came from, it's time to do some digging.

When taking an inventory of debts, list the party to whom it is owed, the amount owed, and whether the debt is secured by a specific asset (e.g., a car loan is secured by the vehicle in question). Common debts to look for include mortgages, credit cards, vehicle loans, and student loans.

Debts that are unsecured (e.g., student loans and credit card debt) are paid from the estate. Secured debts are generally transferred to the person who inherits the asset in question. For example, if the will leaves the car to a particular person, that person also inherits the accompanying car loan.

Credit card companies might cancel some of your spouse's debt, if asked to do so on compassionate grounds. Medical providers might do so as well. Some types of student loans are forgiven upon death. And it never hurts to ask to have a balance forgiven or partially forgiven.

In addition, property that you owned jointly with your spouse (or property you own individually) may not have to be used to pay debts that belonged solely to your deceased spouse. And some assets (e.g., your home) may not be reachable by creditors.

Also, claims received beyond a certain deadline may not have to be paid. But again, the details vary by state (both in terms of length of time as well as when the clock starts ticking).

In short, with all debts, be sure to do your research before assuming it must be paid. And don't blindly believe the creditor if they tell you that you are liable for the debt. Speak with an attorney to learn the details if you think any of the above might be relevant.

Don't start distributing assets and paying off debts immediately. If the estate has insufficient funds to pay off all valid debts, there is a specific order (which varies by state) for which debts receive priority. If you pay somebody who is later in the priority list, and the estate is left with insufficient assets to pay the higher-priority parties, those higher priority parties may be able to sue you personally as the PR. Or if you start giving property to beneficiaries named in the will and there turns out to be insufficient assets to pay off all the creditors, you may be personally liable to those creditors. So, a full inventory of all the assets and debts must be taken before any major payments are made. (Payment of the estate's debts and distribution of remaining assets will be covered later, in Chapter 7.)

One noteworthy exception: for a mortgage or car loan, continue making timely payments. You don't want to default and have to deal with the various repercussions. After the home or vehicle is distributed to the appropriate beneficiary though, that beneficiary will generally be the party responsible for paying that debt.

You will also need to determine the value of all assets included in the estate, in order to determine whether federal/state estate tax is owed and to determine whether the estate qualifies for a "small estate" simplified probate process. Another reason that it's important to determine the value of the assets is that beneficiaries need to know the value on the date of death so that they know their new cost basis for tax purposes. (When somebody inherits property, their cost basis in the inherited property is generally "stepped up to" the fair market value on the date of the original owner's death. Appendix A has more information.) For real estate, an appraisal soon after your spouse's death is fine. But for stock holdings, for example, you will want to look up the actual value on that specific date.

Collect Any Money Owed to the Estate

The PR also has the responsibility of collecting any money owed to the estate. Any such money collected should be deposited directly into the bank account that you set up for the estate.

If you know of any debts that were owed to your spouse, it's your responsibility to collect these, pursuant to the existing terms. For example, if your spouse had made a loan to somebody, and that person was paying your spouse back according to a specific schedule, it's your responsibility to continue to collect the regularly scheduled payments on behalf of the estate.

It's also a good idea to check unclaimed.org and missingmoney.com to check for any unclaimed property in your spouse's name.

Take Notes!

Again, it's important to take notes, not just for the sake of your own sanity but also to protect yourself from various potential sources of legal trouble.

Keep records of anything that you do and your reasons for doing such (e.g., any investment decisions made regarding estate assets).

Chapter 4 Simple Summary

- If you are named as personal representative in the will (or there was no will) and you want to serve as PR, request that the court appoint you as such.

- As the PR of the estate, you have a fiduciary duty to the estate's creditors and beneficiaries. You must put their interests before your own, and you must take prudent care of the assets.

- You will probably need to get a taxpayer ID for the estate and open a bank account for the estate.

- As PR you are responsible for taking an inventory of the estate's assets and debts.

- As PR you are responsible for collecting any money owed to the estate.

CHAPTER FIVE

Updating Your Own Estate Plan

There are a number of documents and accounts that will have to be updated as a result of the death of your spouse.

Updating Important Estate Planning Documents

It's important to update your major estate planning documents, such as your will, living will, and medical and financial powers of attorney. If you don't already have those documents prepared, it's likely that the death of your spouse has illustrated why it's important to have them.

And just to make one point especially clear: if you have minor children or an adult disabled child, it's now critical to create a will that names a guardian for them in the event of your death.

Updating Beneficiary Designations

For your own retirement accounts—as well as any retirement accounts you have inherited from your spouse—it is important to update the primary and contingent beneficiary designations. (The contingent beneficiary is the person to whom the account will pass if the primary beneficiary is no longer alive at the time of your death.) A critical point here is that if a beneficiary is named on an account, the account goes to that beneficiary, regardless of what is stated in your will. Just to repeat this important point: a beneficiary designation overrides whatever is stated in the will.

If multiple primary beneficiaries are named and one of them is already deceased at the time of your death, the default result is that the assets will pass to the other named primary beneficiary. If you want assets to pass to the children of a beneficiary if that beneficiary is no longer alive, you can use a **per stirpes** designation. (Per stirpes is Latin for "by branch.")

EXAMPLE: Darnell has a son and a daughter, each of whom has two children. Darnell names his kids as beneficiaries of his IRA, with each designated to receive 50% of the account. However, by the time of

Darnell's death, Darnell's' daughter has already died. The usual result would be Darnell's son inheriting the entire IRA, rather than 50% going to his son and 50% going to the deceased daughter's children. If Darnell's IRA beneficiary designations were per stirpes, Darnell's son would inherit 50% of the IRA, and his daughter's two children would each inherit 25%.

Rather than directly naming any minor as a beneficiary, you may want to name a trust as beneficiary to manage assets on behalf of the minor. But be sure to consult with a qualified attorney. Depending on the specific terms of the trust, naming the trust as beneficiary of a retirement account may result in undesirable consequences with regard to distributions that would have to be taken from the account.

Similarly, it's important to update the beneficiaries named on any insurance policies that you own that have a death benefit (i.e., life insurance and some types of annuities).

Finally, you may want to consider adding transfer-on-death or payable-on-death beneficiary designations to other assets such as bank or brokerage accounts.

Chapter 5 Simple Summary

- It's important to update your will, living will, and medical and financial powers of attorney to reflect your new circumstances. Or, if you do not have such documents prepared, it's now more important than ever to have them prepared.

- Be sure to update the beneficiary designations on your retirement accounts and insurance policies. You may also want to add transfer-on-death or payable-on-death beneficiary designations to your other assets.

PART TWO

Intermediate Next Steps

CHAPTER SIX

Social Security Planning

As a surviving spouse, there are a few types of Social Security benefits that may be relevant to you in the near future: the lump sum death benefit, child benefits, mother/father benefits, and widow-(er) benefits.

But first we need to back up a step. In order to understand any discussion of Social Security benefits, you need to be familiar with two terms:

- full retirement age (FRA), and
- primary insurance amount (PIA).

Your **full retirement age** is somewhere from age 66 to 67, depending on the year you were born. Your **primary insurance amount** is the amount of retirement benefits you would receive per month if you started taking them at your full retirement age. We won't dig into the details here, but your PIA is determined by your earnings history. (The higher your earnings over the course of your career, the higher your PIA.)

Lump Sum Death Benefit

Social Security will pay you a one-time "lump-sum death benefit" of $255. This obviously isn't much, but there's no reason not to take it. As discussed in Chapter 3, the SSA is one of the first parties to notify of your spouse's death.

Child Benefits

Please note: if you have no minor children or adult disabled children, feel free to skip to the heading "Widow(er) Benefits" later in this chapter.

The children of people who have died may be eligible for a Social Security benefit of their own. To be eligible for such benefits, a child must:

1. Have been a dependent of the deceased,[1]
2. Be the child, legally adopted child, or step-child of the deceased,
3. Be unmarried, and

---

[1] The definition of "dependent" in this context is not the same definition that's used for tax purposes. See Code of Federal Regulations sections 404.360-404.365: ssa.gov/OP_Home/cfr20/404/404-0000.htm

4. Be under age 18, under age 19 and in school full-time in grade 12 or below, or disabled with a disability that began before age 22.

A child benefit on a deceased person's work record is calculated as 75% of the deceased person's primary insurance amount.

When you apply for child benefits on behalf of your child, you will also need to apply to be your child's "representative payee." The representative payee is the party who actually receives the payment, when the beneficiary is unable to manage his/her own benefits due to age or disability.

As representative payee, you have certain responsibilities, such as:

- You must use the use the benefits to pay for the current and future needs of the beneficiary,
- You must save any benefits not needed to meet current needs, and
- You must keep a record of the expenses for which you used the benefit payments.

Many parents of children receiving child benefits decide to save the child's benefits in a custodial account, with the idea being that the money will eventually be used to pay for college. But beware that this decision can backfire. Firstly, at a certain age (usually 18 or 21, depending on the state), the child will get unrestricted access to the account, and they'll be able to spend it as they please. Second, the child's assets are likely to have a more detrimental effect than parental assets on the financial aid they receive for college. In many cases, it will be better to use the child benefits for current expenses to support the child (clothes, food, etc.) and then have more of your own assets available when the time comes in order to pay for college.

One quick warning about taxes as a representative payee: do *not* report the child's benefit payments as your own income, even though the payments were made into your own bank account. It's still the child's income. (And in most cases, the income will be tax-free to your child.)

Mother/Father Benefits

You will generally be eligible for mother/father benefits on your deceased spouse's work record if:

1. You have not remarried;
2. You have a child in your care who is a) under 16 or disabled and b) entitled to benefits on your deceased spouse's work record; and
3. You have not yet applied for your regular widow/widower benefit (i.e., your surviving spouse benefit).

The amount of a mother/father benefit is 75% of your deceased spouse's primary insurance amount.

Conversion to Widow(er) Benefits

When you reach your full retirement age, if you are
receiving a mother/father benefit at that time, you
will automatically be "deemed" to have filed for
your widow(er) benefit. And because of eligibility
requirement #3 discussed above, this means your
mother/father benefit will terminate at that time.

Widow(er) Benefits

Please note: if a) you are not disabled and you are
much younger than age 60 or b) you are disabled
and you are much younger than age 50, feel free to
skip to the heading "Reductions to Various Benefits" later in this chapter, as the following few sections about widow(er) benefits are not going to be
relevant to you for quite some time.

In most cases, you will be eligible for
widow(er) benefits if:

- The marriage lasted at least nine months[1],
- You are at least 60 years old (or disabled and
  at least age 50), and
- You have not remarried, unless you remarried *after* reaching age 60.

---

[1] A common misconception is that the marriage must
have lasted 10 years. The 10-year requirement is for receiving benefits on an ex-spouse's record after divorce.

Calculation of Widow(er) Benefits

Assuming that you have reached full retirement age by the time you claim widow(er) benefits:

- If your spouse died *prior* to full retirement age without having filed for retirement benefits, your widow(er) benefit will be 100% of your deceased spouse's primary insurance amount.
- If your spouse died *after* reaching full retirement age without having filed for retirement benefits, your widow(er) benefit will be equal to the amount your deceased spouse would have received if he/she had filed on the date of death.
- If your spouse was already receiving benefits by the time of death, your widow(er) benefit will be equal to the greater of a) the amount your deceased spouse was receiving prior to death or b) 82.5% of your deceased spouse's primary insurance amount.

EXAMPLE: Lynn dies at age 63, having never filed for her own retirement benefit. Lynn's husband Hank (who has already reached full retirement age) immediately claims a widower's benefit. Hank's widower's benefit will be 100% of Lynn's primary insurance amount, because she died prior to reaching her FRA and she had not yet filed for her retirement benefit.

Conversely, if Lynn died at age 69 not yet having filed for her retirement benefit, Hank's widower's benefit would be equal to the amount that Lynn would have received if she had filed for her benefit on her date of death (which would be greater than her primary insurance amount, because she was older than full retirement age).

EXAMPLE: Henry has a full retirement age of 67. He claims his retirement benefit at age 64, meaning his retirement benefit is 80% of his primary insurance amount.

Henry then dies at age 65. His wife Wanda (who has already reached full retirement age) claims a widow's benefit immediately. Wanda's widow's benefit will be 82.5% of Henry's PIA (because she gets the greater of 82.5% or the amount he was receiving, which was 80%).

EXAMPLE: Harry claims his retirement benefit at age 68, then dies at age 69. Harry's wife Rita (who has already reached full retirement age) claims a widow's benefit immediately. Rita's widow's benefit will be equal to the benefit that Harry had been receiving at the time of his death (which will be greater than Harry's primary insurance amount, because he claimed after full retirement age).

Like retirement benefits and spousal benefits, widow(er) benefits are adjusted for inflation. This inflation adjustment includes any time between the date at which the first spouse dies and the date at which the surviving spouse claims a widow(er)'s benefit.

EXAMPLE: Wendy files for retirement benefits at age 65, then dies at 66. Her husband Howard is 60 years old at the time of Wendy's death. Seven years later, at his full retirement age, Howard files for widower benefits. He'll receive the amount that Wendy was receiving, adjusted for any inflation that occurred over the seven intervening years.

Claiming Widow(er) Benefits Prior to Full Retirement Age

If you claim widow(er) benefits *prior* to reaching full retirement age, the amount received will be reduced. Widow(er) benefits claimed at age 60 (the minimum age for widow(er) benefits) will be equal to 71.5% of the amount that would have been received if claimed at full retirement age.[1]

EXAMPLE: June dies at age 63, having never filed for benefits. As discussed previously, this means

[1] Exception: If your spouse had claimed retirement benefits prior to FRA and you claim your widow(er) benefit prior to FRA, your widow(er) benefit will be greater than what the above would indicate. See Appendix B for details.

that if her husband Frank claims his widower's benefit at full retirement age, he will receive an amount equal to June's primary insurance amount. If Frank claims at age 60, however, he will only receive 71.5% of June's primary insurance amount.

The reduction in widow(er) benefits decreases proportionately as you near full retirement age. So, for example, if you claim widower benefits halfway between age 60 and full retirement age, the amount received will be 85.75% (that is, halfway between 71.5% and 100%) of the amount that would have been received at FRA.

Deemed Filing Doesn't Apply to Widow(er) Benefits

When it comes to *spousal* benefits and retirement benefits, if you are eligible for both and you file for one or the other, you'll automatically be "deemed" to have filed for the other. But this deemed filing rule does *not* apply to widow(er) benefits. As a result, there are two possible Social Security claiming strategies that often make sense for somebody whose spouse has passed away:

1. At age 60, you claim a widow(er) benefit while allowing your own retirement benefit to grow until 70, or

2. You claim your own retirement benefit at 62 while allowing your widow(er) benefit to grow until full retirement age.

The first thing you'll want to do is calculate your maximum widow(er) benefit (i.e., your widow(er) benefit if you wait until full retirement age to claim it) and your maximum retirement benefit (i.e., your retirement benefit if you wait until age 70 to claim it). Alternatively, you can call the SSA and ask them to calculate these two amounts for you. Whichever of those two amounts is smaller is typically the benefit that you should claim as early as possible, while you then allow the other benefit to grow until it maxes out (either at FRA or at age 70, depending upon which benefit it is).

One noteworthy exception to the above strategy is that if you are younger than full retirement age and still working, the Social Security earnings test could result in your retirement benefit or widow(er) benefit being completely withheld anyway. In such a situation, it usually makes sense to wait to file for benefits. Depending on how the math works out, the ideal month to file could be January of the year in which you stop working, the month in which you stop working, January of the year you reach full retirement age, or the month you reach full retirement age.[1]

---

[1] An online calculator such as OpenSocialSecurity.com can do this math for you.

Reductions to Various Benefits

There are other factors that could result in reduction of your mother/father benefit, your widow(er) benefit, or your child's child benefit.

- If you are working and younger than full retirement age, the Social Security earnings test could result in your mother/father benefit or widow(er) benefit being partially or fully withheld.
- If you are receiving a government pension from work that was not covered by Social Security tax, the "government pension offset" will reduce your mother/father benefit or widow(er) benefit by 2/3 of your monthly pension amount.
- If more than one child is receiving child benefits on your deceased spouse's work record, the family maximum rule could result in reduction of any benefits on that work record (i.e., the child benefits and your mother/father benefit or widow(er) benefit).
- If you have applied for your own retirement benefit, your mother/father benefit or widow(er) benefit will be reduced (but not below zero) by the amount of your retirement benefit.

Of note: *unlike* most types of Social Security benefits, mother/father benefits are not reduced as a result of filing for them prior to your full retirement age. Point being, if you are eligible for a mother/father benefit, it usually makes sense to file for it as soon as possible.

Retroactive Applications

When you file for any type of benefit (retirement benefit, mother/father benefit, widow(er) benefit, spousal benefit, or child benefit) you can backdate your application by up to 6 months, subject to two limitations.

First, you cannot backdate an application to a date prior to the point at which you became eligible for the benefit. So you cannot, for example, backdate an application for widow(er) benefits to a month prior to the month in which your spouse died.

Second, applications for widow(er) benefits, retirement benefits, and spousal benefits cannot usually be backdated to a month earlier than the month in which you reach your full retirement age. There are two exceptions for widow(er) benefits though. Firstly, if your spouse died last month, your application can be made retroactive to last month, even if you're younger than full retirement age. Second, if your spouse had filed for his/her retirement benefit prior to his/her full retirement age, a retroactive application for widow(er) benefits might be an option for you.

Chapter 6 Simple Summary

- If you have a minor child or adult disabled child, he/she may be able to receive a child's benefit on your spouse's work record.

- If you have a child in your care who is under 16 or disabled, you may be able to receive a mother/father benefit on your spouse's record.

- If you are at least age 60, you may be able to receive a widow(er) benefit on your spouse's work record.

- Various reductions (e.g., the earnings test if you're still working, or the family maximum if you have a child receiving child benefits) can apply to most types of Social Security benefits.

- A filing strategy that often makes sense for surviving spouses is to file for their smaller benefit (either a widow(er) benefit or their own retirement benefit) as early as possible, while allowing the other benefit to grow until it maxes out.

CHAPTER SEVEN

Further Responsibilities as Personal Representative

As the personal representative of the estate, after taking an inventory of the estate's assets and liabilities (discussed in Chapter 4), it will be time to pay the estate's debts and distribute any remaining property to the appropriate beneficiaries.

Pay Creditors

If you're going through a formal probate process, you may need the judge's permission before you can start paying the estate's debts. If the estate has sufficient assets to pay all of the debts that you have determined to be valid, the probate court will approve you to pay all of those debts. If the estate does not have sufficient assets to pay all of its valid debts, you will proceed through the list, paying them off in order of priority (as determined by your state) until the assets are depleted.

Distribute Remaining Property

After all creditors have been paid and the deadline for new creditor claims has passed, distribute any remaining property as per the will—or as per the court's direction, if your spouse died without a will. (Some states may require you to request the court's permission to distribute the remaining property.)

If the estate includes any firearms or other heavily regulated property (e.g., cannabis), be very careful that you are not violating any federal or state laws by transferring such property to beneficiaries. For example, a firearm cannot be distributed to a convicted felon, regardless of what the will says.

Close the Estate

After creditors have been paid and the estate's assets have been distributed, you can close the estate. To close the estate, you will likely have to provide the court with documentation of the income the estate received, expenses the estate incurred, assets that were paid to creditors, and assets that were distributed to beneficiaries. Once the estate has been closed, the probate process is formally over, and

you are finished with your duties as personal representative.

You should also file another Form 56 with
the IRS to let them know that you will no longer be
acting as a fiduciary for the estate.

Again, it varies by state, but the estate will
probably need to remain open for at least 6 months,
in order to give creditors the required length of time
to submit a claim against the estate. And in many
cases, the estate will remain open in excess of one
year—or possibly multiple years in the case of a
complex estate or feuding beneficiaries.

Take Notes!

Once again, it's critical to take notes about any actions you take on behalf of the estate (e.g., distributions of property) and your reasons for taking those
actions.

Chapter 7 Simple Summary

- Consult with an attorney if you don't think the estate will have sufficient assets to pay all of its debts or if you have questions about whether the estate or you personally are liable for a particular debt.

- As personal representative you are responsible for paying the estate's valid debts and distributing any remaining assets according to the will or state intestate succession rules.

- After creditors have been given the required length of time to submit a claim, valid debts have been paid, and any remaining assets have been distributed, you can close the estate. To close the estate you will likely have to provide the court with an accounting of income, expenses, and distributions. Once the estate has been closed, the probate process is over.

CHAPTER EIGHT

Handling Inherited Retirement Accounts

When you inherit an IRA, 401(k), or other employer-sponsored retirement account from your spouse, the most immediate concern is whether a required minimum distribution (RMD) has to be taken for this year.[1] If your spouse was old enough for RMDs to be required (generally age 72), and he/she had not yet taken the necessary RMD for the year of death, that RMD becomes the responsibility of the beneficiary. If there are multiple beneficiaries, the RMD can be split among them in any way.

---

[1] This chapter assumes that you are already familiar with the basic rules regarding retirement accounts (i.e., before they're inherited). If you need an intro to IRAs in general, IRS Publication 590-A (regarding contributions to the accounts) and 590-B (regarding distributions from the accounts) are a good place to start.

EXAMPLE: María dies at age 75, having not yet taken her RMD from her traditional IRA this year. The account is left to three beneficiaries. As long as the three beneficiaries, in total, take distributions at least equal to María's RMD for this year, the IRS will be satisfied.

After the year-of-death RMD has been satisfied (if necessary), you have three primary options as a spousal beneficiary:

1. Disclaim (i.e., elect *not* to inherit) the account—an option that we'll discuss in the next chapter;
2. Roll the assets into your own IRA; or
3. Leave the assets in the inherited IRA in your spouse's name (or if the inherited account was a 401(k) or similar, roll the assets into an inherited IRA).

If a party other than you was also named as a beneficiary of the account, stricter RMD rules will apply. However, those stricter rules can often be circumvented (thereby allowing you to use the normal rules for a spousal beneficiary) if any non-human beneficiaries receive their share of the account by September 30 of the year following the year of death and the account is split into separate accounts for each human beneficiary by the end of the year following the year of death. If this situation applies to you, consulting with a tax professional who has experience in these matters is definitely a good idea.

Spousal Rollover

If you roll the assets into your own IRA, from that point forward it's just a normal IRA (i.e., it's just like any other IRA that was yours to begin with), so all the normal IRA rules apply, whether Roth or traditional.

If you already have an IRA of your own, rolling the assets into your own IRA can be helpful from a simplification point of view (i.e., consolidating assets into a smaller number of accounts).

An important point is that there's no deadline on a spousal rollover. Should you want to, you can own the account as a spousal beneficiary (i.e., leave the assets in the inherited IRA) for several years, then elect to do a spousal rollover.

Own the Account as a Beneficiary

If you continue to own the account as a spousal beneficiary (i.e., you leave the assets in an inherited IRA titled in your spouse's name rather than rolling them into your own IRA), the rules will be similar to normal IRA rules, with a few exceptions.

First, you can take distributions from the account without incurring the 10% penalty, regardless of your age. So if you expect to need the money prior to age 59.5, this is a good reason *not* to go the spousal rollover route—at least not yet. (Again, there's no deadline on a spousal rollover.)

Second, if the inherited account was a Roth IRA, any withdrawals of earnings taken prior to the point at which the original owner would have satisfied the 5-year rule will be subject to income tax (though not the 10% penalty).

Third, you'll have to start taking required minimum distributions in the year in which the deceased account owner would have reached age 72, as opposed to the year in which you reach age 72. If you are older than your deceased spouse, this is advantageous because it puts off RMDs for a longer period of time. If you are younger, it is disadvantageous.

Fourth, once you do have to start taking RMDs from the account, those RMDs will be calculated each year based on your own remaining life expectancy from the "Single Life" table in IRS Publication 590-B, as compared to the "Uniform Lifetime" table that is used during the original account owner's lifetime.[1] This is a disadvantage of owning the account as a beneficiary, because it means that the RMDs from the account will generally be larger than if you roll it into your own IRA.

Update Beneficiaries

As we discussed in Chapter 5, after the death of your spouse, it's important to update the beneficiary designations on your retirement accounts. Note that this includes any inherited accounts that you are choosing to continue to own as a beneficiary.

---

[1] There are two exceptions. First, as noted at the beginning of this chapter: if your spouse was required to take an RMD in the year in which he/she died, but had not yet taken it, you're required to take it for him/her, calculated in the same way it would be if he/she were still alive. Second, for years after the year of death, if your deceased spouse was younger than you, you can look up his/her age instead of your age in the "Single Life" table to calculate the RMD.

Chapter 8 Simple Summary

- In the year of your spouse's death, if he/she needed to take a required minimum distribution from any retirement accounts but had not yet done so, the beneficiary of the account is required to take the RMD for that year, calculated as it would be if your spouse were still alive.

- If you inherit an IRA, you can continue to keep the assets in the inherited IRA, or you can roll the assets into your own IRA. For an inherited employer-sponsored plan account, you can roll the assets into an inherited IRA or you can roll the assets into your own IRA.

- Rolling the assets into your own IRA may be helpful from a simplification point of view (i.e., consolidating accounts). But leaving the assets in an inherited account can be beneficial in some cases as well (e.g., if you expect to need to spend some of the money before age 59.5).

- If you are one of multiple beneficiaries of a retirement account, it's a good idea to consult a tax professional about your options.

CHAPTER NINE

Additional Options as a Beneficiary and Surviving Spouse

As a beneficiary and as a surviving spouse, you have a couple of options available to you that may allow you to legally do something other than what the will and beneficiary designations state, if it makes sense to do so.

Disclaiming Assets

For any would-be inherited asset, a beneficiary has the option to **disclaim** the inheritance. To do so is to essentially say "no thank you" to inheriting that asset.

When you disclaim an asset, you do not get to pick the person to whom it goes. Rather, the asset will pass to whomever is next in line. For instance, if it's an IRA and you are the sole primary beneficiary, the IRA would then pass to the contingent beneficiary. If the property is something left via the will (e.g., a piece of jewelry), the will might designate a contingent beneficiary. For cases in which there is no other named beneficiary, the asset would usually pass to whomever gets the rest of the estate. Identifying who will receive disclaimed assets can be complicated and may warrant the retaining of an attorney or other professional.

You can also *partially* disclaim an asset, if it's something that can be divided. For instance, you could opt to disclaim 75% of a checking account.

Why Would You Disclaim an Asset?

Of course, in most cases, people accept any and all assets that are left to them. But there are cases in which it can make sense to disclaim something.

The first is for tax planning purposes—especially in the case of assets that will result in taxable income, such as a traditional IRA.

EXAMPLE: Included among Isaac's assets at the time of his death is a $200,000 traditional IRA. His wife Molly is listed as the sole primary beneficiary, with their two adult children named as 50/50 contingent beneficiaries. Molly does not really need the money. In addition, her own marginal tax rate is considerably higher than the marginal tax rates of the two children. After consulting with her tax professional, Molly decides to disclaim the IRA, so that it will pass to the two children, thereby allowing the family to achieve some tax savings.

Another reason why you might choose to disclaim an asset is that you feel that doing so would result in a more fair outcome in some way. For example, if you are the primary beneficiary of an account and the contingent beneficiary is somebody whom you feel has been disadvantaged relative to other heirs, you could disclaim the account (or part of it) in order to allow a greater amount to pass to that disadvantaged party.

How to Disclaim an Asset

If you plan to disclaim an asset, contact the party in control of the asset (e.g., the brokerage firm where the IRA is held) to ask what their requirements are. For assets with a named beneficiary, the applicable financial institution may require nothing other than a letter indicating your intention.

If you're intending to disclaim an asset, do not take possession of it or use it for yourself in any way, otherwise you will likely lose the option to disclaim it. Also, under federal tax law and the laws of many states, a disclaimer is only valid if made within 9 months of the date of death.

Claiming the Elective Share

In separate property states (i.e., those that do not have community property laws), a surviving spouse has the option to claim the **elective share** of the estate, rather than what he or she was left in the will.[1] The elective share is a fixed portion of the estate, typically between one third and one half. The idea is to protect spouses from being disinherited (i.e., left out of the will). The specifics, including the requirements that must be met as well as how the elective share is calculated, vary based on state law. But, in short, if you wish that your spouse had left you a larger portion of the assets, speak to an attorney, because you may have some options.

Similarly, for an IRA, if your spouse named some other party (i.e., not you) as the beneficiary of the account, depending on your state's law you may have the right to claim a portion of the account for yourself regardless of the beneficiary designation. For most defined contribution plans such as 401(k) or 403(b) plans, the plan is written in such a way that the surviving spouse is the automatic beneficiary of the account, unless he or she has signed a

---

[1] The reason this concept doesn't exist in community property states is that community property is automatically considered to be owned 50% by each spouse. That is, the surviving spouse *already owns* half of the community property, even if he or she isn't left anything at all in the will.

waiver consenting to some other beneficiary designation.

If you and your spouse entered into a valid marriage agreement (pre- or post-nuptial) and waived your respective rights to the elective share, you may not be able to claim it, unless you choose to challenge the validity of the marriage agreement.

Chapter 9 Simple Summary

- You have the option to disclaim (i.e., not inherit) any asset left to you in the will or via a beneficiary designation. If you do so, the asset passes to whomever is next in line to inherit that particular asset. Be sure not to take control of an asset you intend to disclaim. And make sure the disclaimer is filed within the appropriate time, usually nine months.

- Depending on your state law, you may have the option to claim a larger share of the estate than your spouse left to you in his/her will. Similarly, you may have the option to claim a larger share of your spouse's retirement accounts than was left to you via beneficiary designations.

CHAPTER TEN

Tax Returns

As a surviving spouse (and personal representative, if you are appointed to that role), you will have to file certain tax returns. As a reminder, if you choose to accept the role of PR, you are allowed to hire somebody to prepare those returns.

When looking for tax-related information as a surviving spouse or in your role as PR, you may find IRS Publication 559 to be helpful.

Form 1040
(Final Individual Tax Return)

As the surviving spouse, you must file the final income tax return for your spouse for the year of death as well as any returns from prior years that have not yet been filed. (For example, if your spouse died in February of a given year without yet having filed a return for the prior year, you will have to file his/her return for that prior year as well as the return for the year of death.) The PR shares this responsibility with you. You can file jointly with your spouse for years up to and including the year of death, unless you have remarried before year-end.

This final Form 1040 includes all income your spouse received up until the day of death.

The final tax return is due on the same date it would have been due if the death had not occurred (i.e., typically April 15 of the following year).

Qualifying Surviving Spouse Filing Status

For the two years after your spouse's death, if you have a dependent child you may qualify for the **qualifying surviving spouse** filing status (also known as **qualifying widow(er)** filing status). Filing as qualifying surviving spouse allows you to use the married filing jointly tax brackets and standard deduction.

The general requirements for qualifying surviving spouse filing status are that you must not have remarried, you must have a child you can claim as a dependent, the child must have lived in your home all year other than temporary absences, and you must have paid more than half the cost of keeping up the home for the year. See IRS Publication 501 for more details, as well as exceptions to these requirements.

Form 1041
(Income Tax Return for the Estate)

For each year that the estate remains open, the PR also must file an income tax return (Form 1041) for the estate if the estate has $600 or more of gross income. Broadly speaking, the estate has to pay tax each year on any income it receives that is not distributed to beneficiaries. Form 1041 is where all such income and distributions are reported and where the resulting income tax is calculated.

Unless you elect to use a taxable year other than the calendar year for the estate, Form 1041 for each year will be due April 15 of the following year. If you are considering using a taxable year that ends in a month other than December, be sure to consult with a tax professional, because things can get complicated quickly.

Income in respect of a decedent is the technical term for income that a deceased person would have received if the death had not occurred. As noted above, any such income received by the estate is included in the estate's income on Form 1041 (though the estate receives a deduction for any such income distributed to a beneficiary). If a beneficiary receives such income (either as a distribution from the estate, or directly from the payor if the estate has already been closed), it will be included in that beneficiary's gross income.

83

EXAMPLE: After Jack's death, his employer pays his last two weeks of wages into a checking account that the PR established for the estate. Those wages will be taxable as income to the estate, as income in respect of a decedent. However, if the wages are distributed from the estate to the appropriate beneficiaries, the estate will receive a deduction for the distributions and the income will be taxable to the beneficiaries.

Form 706 (Estate Tax Return)

Form 706 is the estate tax return. That is, it's the return relating to the federal estate tax (filed once), whereas Form 1041 discussed above is the income tax return for the estate (filed every year until the estate is closed).

Form 706 generally only has to be filed if one of two things is true:

1. The gross estate, plus taxable gifts made during the person's lifetime (i.e., gifts beyond the annual gift tax exclusion amount) exceed the estate tax exclusion ($12.06 million for 2022; currently scheduled to be reduced by half on January 1, 2026); or
2. The personal representative elects to transfer the deceased spouse's unused estate tax exclusion amount to the surviving spouse.

If Form 706 must be filed, the personal representative must file by 9 months from the date of death, with a 6-month extension possible.

State Returns

In addition to the above, there will generally be forms to file at the state level as well, such as an income tax return for the decedent and income tax return for the estate. As personal representative you may also have to file an estate tax return or inheritance tax return if the state imposes either of those types of tax. (Among the states that impose an estate tax, the threshold is often much lower than the federal estate tax threshold.)

Chapter 10 Simple Summary

- Both the personal representative and surviving spouse have a responsibility to file the final Form 1040 for the deceased in the year of death. You can file jointly with your spouse in the year of death.

- If you have a child, you may be able to use the qualifying surviving spouse filing status for the two years after the year in which your spouse died.

- For each year the estate remains open, the PR must file Form 1041 if the estate has $600 or more of gross income.

- Form 706 is the form used for reporting estate tax or for electing to transfer the decedent's unused exclusion amount to the surviving spouse. Filing Form 706 is the personal representative's responsibility.

- Your state will also likely require a final income tax return for the year of death, as well as an income tax return for the estate for any years that it remains open. You may also have to file additional paperwork if your state imposes an estate or inheritance tax.

CHAPTER ELEVEN

Reassessing Your Own Finances

Much as you did for the estate (if you're the personal representative), it's now time to take an inventory of your own financial picture, as it stands at this point. Specifically, you will want to calculate three things:

1. Your assets,
2. Your new level of income, and
3. Your new monthly and annual expenses.

Ultimately the goal is to determine whether the new rate of spending is sustainable, given the resources available to you.

Inventorying Your Assets and Income

Taking an inventory of your assets should be relatively straightforward, once the estate has been settled and you know which assets are available to you, as opposed to going to other beneficiaries.

When inventorying your assets, we're particularly concerned with *financial* assets (i.e., assets from which you can spend—bank accounts, brokerage accounts, etc.). You do not, for example, need to spend time determining the value of your car, unless you're planning to sell that car and use the proceeds for spending.

When inventorying your income, you'll want to include your own earnings, any Social Security income, and any income from pensions or annuities. At this point, do not include any interest or dividend income from the portfolio. (As we'll discuss momentarily, the rate at which you can spend from a portfolio is not really a function of the amount of interest or dividends it provides.)

Estimating Expenses

After taking an inventory of your assets and income, the next step is to determine your current rate of spending. It's important to determine not just a monthly spending figure but also an annual spending figure. Because many expenses do not occur every month, looking only at a particular month and just multiplying by twelve may give an annual figure that is very different than your actual annual spending.

To calculate your expenses over the last year, you'll need three things: credit card statements, bank statements, and payroll stubs for both you and your spouse (for expenses like insurance that were deducted directly from wages). When tallying your expenses, be sure to include any debt-servicing payments (mortgage payment, car payment, student loan payment, etc.).

After calculating your expenses for the last year, do your best to adjust for amounts that will be different after the loss of your spouse. For example, food, health insurance, and health care costs will be less. Conversely, there may be some new costs (e.g., if you will now have to pay for childcare).

What's Sustainable?

Again, the goal of this whole exercise (inventorying assets, liabilities, and income and then determining your new rate of spending) is to see whether your rate of spending is sustainable or whether any adjustments need to be made. Generally, you can think of the sustainable rate of spending as your current reliable sources of income, plus a certain rate of spending from any portfolio assets.

Determining a reasonable rate of spending from assets depends primarily on how long you want those assets to last. If the idea is for them to just get you through the next few years, until you find a job that pays more, spending at a very high rate is reasonable—and you may have no other choice. Or, if the plan is to spend them down entirely over eight years of paying for college education, then simple arithmetic tells us that you can spend about 1/8th (12.5%) of the assets each year. Alternatively, if you're retired at 60 years old, and these assets may have to last you 3-4 decades, a much lower rate of spending will be necessary.

If you search online for "sustainable spending rate" you'll find a mountain of research, articles, and debate over how much can safely be spent per year from a retirement portfolio. There's also quite a bit of debate over *how* to spend from a retirement portfolio. (For example, should you pick a given percentage, and then spend that same percentage each year, thereby allowing your spending to fluctuate up and down with the portfolio's performance? Or should you pick a given dollar amount and keep spending that same dollar amount every year?) Suffice to say that this is a major simplification, but a rough guideline is that as long as a significant part of the portfolio is invested in stocks, spending about 3-4% per year from a retirement portfolio is probably reasonable—closer to 4% if you're of typical retirement age and closer to 3% if you're an early retiree.[1]

Making Adjustments

If your new projected level of spending does not look sustainable, you'll have to make adjustments—either figuring out where to cut costs, figuring out how to increase your income, or both.

With regard to cutting costs, having just made an inventory of exactly what you are spending will be helpful. Take some time to identify any on-going spending items that you don't think are necessary. And take some time to identify the largest items and think about whether anything can be done to scale those back.

Small changes can add up, but most people will find that there's one change that has the largest potential to make an impact: downsizing your home. This would obviously be a major life change. But in some cases, that's what's necessary.

Or, if you are retired, you own your home, and you don't want to sell it, a reverse mortgage can

---

[1] The following articles may be of interest if you're looking for more discussion on these topics:
https://obliviousinvestor.com/there-is-no-perfect-retire-ment-spending-strategy/
https://obliviousinvestor.com/an-ideal-retirement-spending-strategy/

be a good option for raising funds for living expenses. But be sure that you understand how a reverse mortgage works before going that route.[1]

Increasing your income could mean increasing your hours at work. It could mean working toward (and explicitly requesting) a raise. If you are retired or you have been a full-time parent, it could mean going back into the workforce. It could mean a career change. Like downsizing your home, most of these things are major undertakings. But they might be necessary.

---

[1] Wade Pfau's book *Reverse Mortgages: How to use Reverse Mortgages to Secure Your Retirement* is an excellent resource on the topic of reverse mortgages.

Chapter 11 Simple Summary

- It's important to determine whether your new rate of spending is sustainable, given your assets and income.

- Step one is to take an inventory of the net assets available to you (i.e., assets minus liabilities), as well as your new level of income.

- Next, you'll want to calculate your new projected rate of spending. It's important to do an annual calculation here, rather than just looking at the last month and multiplying by twelve.

- The appropriate rate of spending from a portfolio of assets depends primarily on how long you want those assets to last. For a retirement portfolio, an annual spending rate of 3-4% is often considered reasonable.

- If you determine that your current level of spending is not sustainable, you will need to make some adjustments. In some cases, major changes such as downsizing your home or making a career change could be necessary.

CHAPTER TWELVE

Reassess Your Portfolio

It's important to reassess your investment portfolio, to see whether it's a fit for your new circumstances. This is important but *probably* not urgent. For example, if you have a lot of uninvested cash from an insurance policy, missing a few months of returns is not a big deal. Take your time with these decisions. If a financial professional tells you that you must hurry, be skeptical. There's a good chance that he or she is just trying to make a sale. The one exception would be that if you find that your portfolio is much too risky (e.g., a large part of the portfolio is invested in a single individual stock), yes, addressing that *is* a high priority.

When building or reworking a portfolio, there are four things you'll want to do:

1. Diversify.
2. Select an appropriate level of risk.
3. Keep costs low.
4. Keep it simple.

Diversify

It's unwise to have a major piece of your portfolio invested in any one stock. And that's doubly true if that stock is the stock of your employer. Perhaps you think that in *your* case it's safe, because this is a company that you know very well and you know that the company has great prospects. But please understand that that's *precisely* what most people are thinking when they have a very large holding of one single stock. And many of those people turn out to be wrong, much to their dismay.

Select an Appropriate Level of Risk

Determining an appropriate level of risk for your portfolio depends on how much risk you can tolerate (psychologically) and how much risk you can afford (financially).

How much risk you can tolerate psychologically depends on your level of experience with investing. If you're new, you're likely to find your first big market downturn scarier than if you've already been through several in your life. Psychological risk tolerance also depends on temperament. Some people are just naturally comfortable with risk. Other people aren't. The goal here is to select an asset allocation for your portfolio (i.e., how much in stocks, how much in bonds) that will allow you to stick with it without feeling panic or high levels of stress when the stock market performs poorly.

How much risk you can *afford* is primarily a function of your flexibility.

EXAMPLE: Patrick's wife Teresa recently died. Teresa had purchased a life insurance policy to provide funds for their son's college education. The son in question is now a senior in high school, which means that the money is going to be entirely spent over the next few years.

There's very little room for risk here. Patrick cannot afford for this money to decline in value, so he needs to pick a safe asset allocation for it.

EXAMPLE: Janice is reevaluating her portfolio after the death of her husband. Janice is 73 years old and retired. Her Social Security benefit and a defined benefit pension cover all of her basic needs, so she's only spending from the portfolio at a very modest rate.

Janice has a lot of flexibility. She can afford to take on a high level of risk in her portfolio, because even a severe market downturn would not be a real problem for her. Conversely, she doesn't *need* a high rate of return, so she could choose a low level of risk, if she wanted. Either decision—or anywhere in between—would be reasonable.

An important point here is that asset allocation is not a precise science, despite what the financial sector may want you to believe. For example, if a 60%-stock, 40%-bond allocation would be suitable for somebody, a 50/50 allocation or 70/30 allocation would also probably be fine. And the other levers that you can adjust (e.g., whether to use exclusively Treasury bonds as opposed to a "total bond market" fund) are even less important.

Keep Costs Low

When it comes to selecting which specific fund(s) you want to use for each part of your portfolio, there are two very important things to know.

First, the way that many people pick mutual funds—selecting one with excellent past performance—doesn't work very well. Picking a particular fund that has a good track record tends to only work about as well as just picking randomly. (If that sounds surprising, I'd encourage you to look up the most recent "Persistence Scorecard" from S&P to see for yourself. They put the report out twice each year, and it consistently shows that picking a fund with excellent past performance is not a particularly reliable way to get excellent performance going forward.)

And second, mutual funds with low expense ratios tend to outperform mutual funds with high expense ratios. For instance, in a 2016 study, Morningstar's Russel Kinnel summarized his findings as follows:

We've done this over many years and many fund types, and expense ratios consistently show predictive power. Using expense ratios to choose funds helped in every asset class and in every quintile from 2010 to 2015. [...] The cheaper the quintile, the better your chances. All told, cheapest-quintile funds were 3 times as likely to succeed as the priciest quintile.

With these two facts in mind, a reasonable way to pick a mutual fund within a given category (e.g., broadly diversified US stock funds) is simply to pick one with a very low expense ratio. Most of the time, this leads to using index funds or ETFs as the building blocks of a portfolio.

Keep It Simple

Simple portfolios offer significant benefits relative to more complicated ones. They're easier to understand. They require less work to manage. In taxable accounts, they require less recordkeeping. Many people find that with a simpler portfolio, they spend less time worrying about whether a particular fund should be swapped out for something else.

Some people have the idea that you need a lot of different funds in order to have a diversified portfolio. That's absolutely false. Having more mutual funds does *not* mean that you're any more diversified. As a CPA I have encountered many people with portfolios that include several mutual funds, all of which own roughly the same underlying investments. The result is that they have a complicated portfolio that's no more diversified than if they just owned one of those funds.

You can create a diversified portfolio using just a single fund, *if* it's the right fund. For example, a balanced fund or a target-date fund would be a one-fund, diversified portfolio. There are some caveats about using such funds though. Firstly, you should make sure that the underlying asset allocation is a good fit for you. (For example, if you look at the underlying asset allocations of all the target-date funds from a given fund company, you might find that the one that best fits your personal risk tolerance is not the one that you would expect based purely on their names.) Second, these all-in-one funds are usually *not* a good fit for taxable accounts, because they're often tax-inefficient (that is, they create relatively high tax costs when held in taxable brokerage accounts). Such funds should generally only be held within retirement accounts such as a 401(k) or IRA.

Or, you can have a very diversified, low-cost, simple portfolio using just two funds (e.g., Vanguard Total World Stock ETF plus a bond fund).

Or you could use a three-fund portfolio (e.g., a US stock fund, an international stock fund, and a bond fund), if you want to adjust the allocation between US stocks and international stocks in some way that is different than what is held by a "total world" fund.

I don't mean to imply that the above suggestions are the only good choices for a portfolio. As we'll discuss next, for any given person there are countless different portfolios that would be acceptable. But please know that including a greater number of funds does not, in itself, make your portfolio any better. In fact it's quite the opposite: all else being equal, the simpler you can make your portfolio, the better.

There Is No Perfect Portfolio

If you ask a dietician what makes a healthy meal, they might give you a list of requirements that need to be satisfied (e.g., a reasonable number of calories, not a ton of sugar, likely includes one or more vegetables, etc.). But there are about a zillion different meals that would meet all of those requirements. There's no single Right Answer.

Creating a portfolio that is suitable for your needs is similar. There are a few boxes that need to be checked (diversified, appropriate risk level, low-cost, and simple enough to manage). But there are a zillion different portfolios that would check all of those boxes.

There is no *perfect* portfolio. But there are many *perfectly fine* portfolios. The goal is to create a portfolio that is "good enough"—and then stop worrying about it.

It's All One Portfolio

When selecting holdings for each account, it can be helpful to keep in mind that all of your various accounts collectively make up one portfolio. And it's the overall portfolio that matters. Point being, there's no need for each individual account to hold a fully diversified asset allocation. It's often simpler for the smaller accounts to hold just a single fund. And then one account (often the biggest one) holds all of the necessary pieces to bring your overall portfolio allocation to your desired target.

EXAMPLE: Richard has decided to use an allocation of 40% U.S. stocks, 20% international stocks, and 40% bonds. His portfolio consists of a taxable brokerage account (which is 10% of his overall portfolio), a Roth IRA (15% of the overall portfolio), and a traditional IRA (75% of the overall portfolio).

Richard can invest the taxable account and Roth IRA entirely in a "total U.S. stock market" index fund and then allocate the traditional IRA as necessary to achieve the overall desired allocation. This way, ongoing management of the portfolio will be kept to the traditional IRA. The taxable account and Roth IRA can be left alone.

Chapter 12 Simple Summary

- A critical requirement for a portfolio is that it must be diversified. However, owning a greater number of mutual funds does not necessarily mean you're any more diversified.

- When selecting an asset allocation for your portfolio, the goal is to end up with something that does not exceed the level of risk you can tolerate psychologically or the level of risk you can afford financially.

- When selecting a mutual fund within a given category (e.g., U.S. stocks), picking based on past performance does not work very well. An approach that is more statistically successful is to simply pick a fund with a very low expense ratio in each category you want to use.

- There is no single best portfolio for any given person. If your portfolio is diversified, has an appropriate level of risk, and is low-cost, it's good enough. If it's simple as well, that's even better.

CHAPTER THIRTEEN

Finding Professional Assistance

As has been stated throughout the book, if you are the personal representative of your spouse's estate, you're allowed to hire professional help such as an attorney and/or tax professional. In addition, your personal circumstances have changed dramatically, and it may be beneficial to hire a financial planner to help you get your own affairs in order. (You may also find that you want to hire a tax professional on your own behalf, if your spouse was the one who prepared your returns every year.)

Engaging an Attorney

With regard to dealing with your spouse's estate, some of the factors that would point in favor of hiring an attorney would include:

- You anticipate that there may be disagreement among the beneficiaries (or among the PRs, if there are more than one).
- You have one or more children with somebody other than your deceased spouse—or he/she had one or more children with somebody other than you.
- There's a question as to the will's validity.
- It's likely that the estate has insufficient assets to pay all of its creditors.
- You are unsure about the validity of certain debts.
- You are considering disclaiming assets or claiming the elective share of the estate as a spouse.
- You and/or your spouse's estate plans include a trust.
- The estate is subject to federal estate tax or your state's estate or inheritance tax.

One easy place to begin the search is simply with a Google search for estate planning attorneys, probate attorneys, or elder law attorneys in your area. The attorney doesn't *necessarily* have to be local, but it's probably a good idea, as somebody local will have better knowledge of your state's laws and your county's probate procedures.

Another good approach is to ask around. Some people you might want to ask for a referral would include:

- Anybody you know who has been through a similar experience (e.g., losing their spouse or serving as PR of an estate).
- Any attorneys you know, with other areas of expertise.
- Any CPAs or other financial professionals you know.

It's critical to find an attorney with the right specialty. An attorney specializing in criminal law, for example, is not going to have the expertise you need. (Though again, such an attorney probably *would* be a good person to email to request a referral to an estates attorney.)

Before officially engaging an attorney, be sure to explicitly ask: what experience do you have in dealing with clients in situations like mine? If you're looking for an attorney to help guide you through the probate process, you want somebody who has done exactly that for many clients.

It's also important to ask about their fees, including questions such as whether the initial consultation is free and what services are included for the stated fee.

If you're working with an attorney who charges hourly, have your records ready at hand and have a list of prepared questions. Being efficient will save you time and money. (Note that the same goes for working with any tax professional or financial planner who charges hourly.)

If your spouse worked with an attorney to prepare his/her will, that attorney could be a good choice, though you are not required to work with that attorney.

Engaging a Tax Professional

You might want to hire a tax professional for assistance with the estate's filing obligations if you're the personal representative. You might want to hire a tax professional for assistance with your own filing obligations (especially if it's something you've never handled before). Or you might want to hire a tax professional for forward-looking tax planning. This person could be a CPA, enrolled agent, or a tax attorney. (Enrolled agents are tax professionals federally licensed by the IRS. To become an enrolled agent, a professional must pass a comprehensive exam covering a wide range of tax-related topics.)

The process for finding a tax professional is similar to the process for finding an attorney. An online search is likely to turn up lots of options. And it's worth asking the same list of people for referrals (i.e., attorneys, financial professionals, and people in your social network who have—or who have been through—similar circumstances). Similarly, you'll want to inquire as to the professional's experience dealing with clients in similar situations, as well as their fees and what is included for those fees.

Finding Financial Advice

When it comes to finding somebody to provide financial advice, the first thing that confuses (and surprises) many people is that the term financial advisor doesn't have any legal meaning at all. Anybody can refer to himself or herself as a financial advisor. A person who refers to himself or herself as a financial advisor might, from a regulatory perspective, actually be any of a few different things: an investment adviser representative, an insurance agent, a registered representative, or none of the above.

Registered Investment Adviser (RIA)

A registered investment adviser (RIA) is an entity (a person or a business) that provides investment advice for a fee. An investment adviser representative (IAR) is a person who works for an RIA and provides advice on behalf of the RIA.

Registered investment advisers (and representatives thereof) have a fiduciary duty to their clients. That is, they're required by law to put the client's interests ahead of their own. Unfortunately, the reality is that there are some RIAs who do not actually live up to a fiduciary standard. So a certain level of self-education is still necessary, in order for you to be able to understand what the advisor is recommending and why.

Registered Representative

A registered representative (also known as a broker or stockbroker) is a salesperson for a broker-dealer (i.e., a brokerage firm). Registered representatives are generally paid a commission. Despite providing advice, they do not (usually) have to be RIAs, because the advice they provide is considered to be solely incidental to the business as a broker (i.e., the business of selling investments).

Though regulation on this topic is currently evolving, in some circumstances registered representatives are only held to a "suitability" standard rather than a fiduciary standard. That is, they are not always required to put the client's interests first.

When you see, "securities offered by...." on a website or other piece of marketing material, you are dealing with a registered representative.

Certified Public Accountant (CPA)

The certified public accountant (CPA) designation is a license (at the state level). But, roughly speaking, the only things that CPAs are allowed to do which other people are not allowed to do are:

- Provide auditing (or similar) services, and
- Use the "CPA" letters after their name.

So if you're looking for personal financial services, it's very unlikely that you *need* somebody who is a CPA. That said, the CPA designation can be relevant, as it means that the person has a certain level of expertise with tax and other financial topics.

Certified Financial Planner (CFP)

The certified financial planner (CFP) designation is not actually a license. The entity that provides this designation (Certified Financial Planner Board of Standards, Inc, generally just referred to as the "CFP Board") is a private entity rather than a governmental entity.

From a legal standpoint, all this designation means is that the person is allowed to use the registered trademark "CFP professional" to describe himself/herself and use the registered trademark "CFP" letters after his/her name.

So from a legal standpoint, this designation is not important at all. That is, there's no service at all for which it's legally necessary for the service provider to be a CFP. However, the CFP designation does mean that the person a) has passed an exam that covers quite a bit of financial planning material and b) has a meaningful amount of experience providing one or more financial planning services.

What Type of Professional is Right for You?

An important point to understand is that somebody can work in more than one of the above roles. For example, it's common to see people who are both IARs and registered representatives. That is, they provide advice for a fee, and they also sell products for a commission. And that person might also have the CPA or CFP designations—or not.

Before searching for individual professionals, take a few minutes to consider three questions:

1. What services do you want?
2. What credentials do you want?
3. How do you want to pay for those services?

Are you looking for comprehensive financial planning? Then it's probably best to find somebody who is an RIA (or representative thereof). The CFP designation (or the CPA designation if you're seeking tax advice) would be great to see. But it isn't entirely necessary.

Are you looking specifically for somebody to do a certain type of tax planning for you? Then a CPA would likely be a good fit. But a CFP could be a great choice as well, if they happen to specialize in that particular area. A tax attorney or enrolled agent could also be a good choice.

And in some related areas—estate planning, for instance—the best professional to work with is probably an attorney.

And finally, just because somebody has the right designation(s) doesn't mean he or she is necessarily a good fit for what you need. Compensation matters as well. For instance, if you're looking for a one-time engagement, you will want to find a professional who *usually* works in such a manner, rather than a professional who prefers to work with clients who have ongoing needs and who are happy to pay an ongoing annual fee.

Chapter 13 Simple Summary

- Hiring an attorney to help with the probate process may be wise, especially if you are unclear as to your rights or obligations.

- Similarly, it may be a good idea to engage a tax professional to help with tax filing obligations (yours or the estate's) and potentially forward-looking tax planning.

- If you're looking for financial planning, it's probably best to work with somebody who is an RIA (or representative thereof), as they will be held to a fiduciary standard. Designations such as CFP or CPA demonstrate a degree of knowledge and experience, but they are not legally necessary.

- Before engaging an attorney, tax professional, or financial planner be sure to ask about their relevant experience and get details as to their fees.

CONCLUSION

What's Next?

In addition to the burden of grief, the death of your spouse imposes a surprisingly large *administrative* burden upon you. There's a lot to do. Notifying a bunch of different entities that your spouse has passed away. Handling the estate administration process. Updating (or creating!) your estate planning documents. Tax filing obligations. Social Security decisions. And taking a step back and looking at your new financial situation, to see what changes need to be made.

But you will get through it. Likely, you've already gotten started. And perhaps you have enlisted professional help or are in the process of doing so.

And again, many of these to-do items are *important* but not *urgent*. One reason I mention that distinction is because many people experience tremendous difficulty concentrating or making decisions (even decisions that would normally be trivially easy) in the period immediately after their spouse's death. For instance, one editor of this book—a highly intelligent and capable human being—reported that shortly after her spouse's death, she found herself feeling overwhelmed in the paper towel aisle at the grocery store, of all places. There were too many choices!

I am not a mental health professional, but I have heard enough similar stories to know that it's a very common experience. The good news is that these people also report that it goes away over time. If you are feeling this way right now, you can be confident that your ability to think clearly and to confidently make decisions will return. For many of the decisions discussed in this book, it's perfectly fine (prudent, even) to give yourself some time for that to occur.

Appendix A

Does an Inheritance Create Taxable Income?

Generally speaking, inheriting an asset does not, in itself, result in any taxable income. For example, inheriting $30,000 in a savings account does not result in $30,000 of taxable income. However, any *earnings* on inherited assets *are* taxable. So if that savings account earns any interest, that interest will be taxable.

When you take money out of a tax-deferred account such as a traditional IRA or 401(k) it is generally taxable as income. And that rule applies just the same for an account beneficiary (i.e., somebody who inherited the account) as it does for the original account owner. One difference is that the 10% penalty that often applies to distributions prior to age 59.5 does not apply if you inherited the account. Please see Chapter 8 for more detail about inherited retirement accounts—the rules and your options.

As discussed in Chapter 10, income in respect of a decedent is the term used for income that a deceased person would have received if the death had not occurred. Such income is taxable to the party that receives it (i.e., the estate or a beneficiary).

When you sell an asset, if the amount you receive from the sale is more than your cost basis, that difference is known as a capital gain, and it is taxable. In most cases, your **cost basis** for an asset is whatever you paid for the asset. If you owned the asset for one year or less prior to selling it, the gain is known as a **short-term capital gain**, and it's taxable at ordinary income tax rates. If you owned the asset for longer than one year prior to selling it, the gain is known as a **long-term capital gain**, and it's taxed at a lower tax rate (often 0% or 15%).

However, when you come into possession of an asset by inheriting it (rather than by buying it), two things happen. Firstly, your cost basis is "stepped up to" the fair market value on the date of the original owner's death. Second, your holding period for the asset is automatically considered to be long-term, even if you sell the asset immediately after inheriting it.

EXAMPLE: Thuy inherits shares of stock from her sister. Her sister paid $5,000 for the shares, and they were worth $26,000 on the date of her death. Thuy sells the shares three months after her sister's death, for $28,000.

Thuy's cost basis in the shares is $26,000, because she received a step-up in cost basis to the fair market value on the date of death. So her capital gain on the sale is just $2,000. And it's a long-term capital gain, because the shares are considered to be long-term property, even though Thuy had owned them for less than one year.

Unless you live in a community property state, if you own property jointly with your spouse and then your spouse dies, you get a half step-up in cost basis. The idea here is that each of you is considered to have owned half of the property, so you get a step-up for the half that your spouse owned and which you have inherited.

EXAMPLE: Kelly buys a piece of real estate with her husband Zach. They pay $300,000 for the property. Years later, Zach dies, leaving Kelly as the sole owner. At the time of Zach's death, the property is worth $500,000.

After Zach's death, Kelly's basis in the property is $400,000. Rather than receiving a *full* step-up in basis (i.e., from $300,000 to $500,000), she received a *half* step-up.

In community property states, the surviving spouse generally receives a *full* step-up in cost basis for community property. So in the above example, if Zach and Kelley lived in California (a community property state) and the real estate was owned as community property, Kelly's new basis would be $500,000.

Capital Gain from Selling Your Home

It's common for surviving spouses to consider selling their home after the death of their spouse. If you have a capital gain from selling your home, you may be able to exclude (that is, not pay tax on) a significant portion of that gain. In order to qualify for this exclusion, you must meet three requirements:

1. For the two years prior to the date of sale, you did not exclude gain from the sale of another home.
2. During the five years prior to the date of sale, you owned the home for at least two years.
3. During the five years prior to the date of sale, you lived in the home as your main home for at least two years.

Note that, for requirements #2 and #3, the two-year time periods do not necessarily have to be made up of 24 consecutive months. Also, if you have not remarried as of the date of sale, you can count any months in which your late spouse owned and lived in the home, even if you did not live there.

The amount of gain that can be excluded is normally $250,000 for a person who is not married. However, as a surviving spouse, you can qualify for a $500,000 exclusion if all of the following are true:

- You sell the home within two years of the date of death.

- You haven't remarried as of the date of sale.
- Neither you nor your deceased spouse used this same sale-of-home exclusion during the two-year period before the date of this sale.

Estate and Inheritance Taxes

In addition to income tax, there are also estate and inheritance taxes that depend on the size of the estate. The federal estate tax applies when the gross estate, plus taxable gifts made during the person's lifetime (i.e., gifts beyond the annual gift tax exclusion amount) exceeds the applicable threshold ($12,060,000 for 2022, currently scheduled to be reduced by half on January 1, 2026).

In addition, some states impose an estate tax, inheritance tax, or both. In some cases, the threshold for a state's estate tax is *much* lower than the federal threshold. While estate taxes are determined by the size of the estate and are paid from the estate's assets, inheritance taxes are imposed on the beneficiary and are paid from the beneficiary's inheritance.

There is generally no estate tax due on the portion of an estate inherited by a spouse who is a U.S. citizen.

Simple Summary

- For the most part, inherited assets are not considered to be taxable income. Similarly, life insurance death benefits are not taxable as income.

- Distributions from tax-deferred accounts (e.g., a traditional IRA) are generally taxable, and that goes for inherited tax-deferred accounts as well.

- When somebody inherits an asset, their cost basis in that asset is usually "stepped up to" (i.e., set equal to) the market value on the date of the owner's death.

- If two spouses jointly own property, when one dies the surviving spouse will generally receive a *half* step-up in cost basis. In community property states, the surviving spouse generally receives a full step-up in cost basis.

- Estate and/or inheritance taxes may be due when somebody other than a U.S. citizen spouse inherits a portion of an estate.

Appendix B

Social Security Widow(er) Benefit Math Details

As discussed in Chapter 6, if you claim a Social Security widow(er) benefit prior to your full retirement age, the amount you receive will be reduced. If your spouse either a) had *not* claimed his/her retirement benefit by the date of death or b) had claimed his/her retirement benefit, but did so after reaching full retirement age, then your widow(er) benefit will be reduced by 28.5% if you claim your widow(er) benefit as early as possible (at age 60). And the amount you receive will increase from there on a pro-rata basis for each month closer you are to full retirement age when you claim widow(er) benefits.

EXAMPLE: Cynthia dies at age 71, having filed for her retirement benefit at age 68. As discussed previously, this means that if her husband Mark claims his widower's benefit at full retirement age, he will receive an amount equal to the monthly retirement benefit that Cynthia was receiving. If Mark claims at age 60, however, he will only receive 71.5% of that amount.

However, if your spouse *had* claimed his/her retirement benefit prior to full retirement age, the calculation is different. The starting point for the calculation is now your deceased spouse's PIA rather than the amount that he/she was receiving at death. From there, the same reduction for early filing (e.g., 28.5% if claimed at age 60) will apply. However, the resulting benefit is then limited to the greater of:

- 82.5% of your deceased spouse's PIA, or
- The amount your deceased spouse was receiving at the time of his/her death.

That's a lot of math. The big takeaway here is that filing early for a widow(er) benefit results in a reduction to that benefit. But if your spouse had filed early for his/her own retirement benefit, then your widow(er) benefit will actually max out *before* you reach your FRA. (Exactly when it maxes out depends on how early your spouse filed.)

Simple Summary

- If you file early for your widow(er) benefit, that benefit will be reduced.

- However, if your spouse had already filed for his/her own retirement benefit and did so prior to reaching his/her full retirement age, then your widow(er) benefit will actually max out prior to your full retirement age.

Appendix C

Dealing with Trusts

As a surviving spouse, you might have to deal with one or more trusts. There are many different types of trusts, each of which serves a particular purpose. The basic idea though is that a trust is a legal entity which can own assets. Sometimes trusts are used for tax planning purposes. In most cases though, the purpose is to allow the person who created the trust to exert some control over how their assets will be managed after their death or incapacitation. That is, somebody can create a trust, fund it with assets, and write the terms of the trust in such a way as to stipulate certain requirements as to how the assets will be invested or spent—and then those rules will have to be followed even after the person who created the trust dies or becomes incapacitated.

With trusts, it's important to get guidance from an attorney who specializes in estate planning. If the attorney is not a tax expert, it will also be critical to get guidance from a tax professional with expertise in estate planning, as there are both income tax and estate/gift tax considerations involved with trusts.

In order to understand the various purposes for a trust and what your rights and responsibilities relating to the trust might be, you need to know a bit of terminology.

Parties to a Trust

A trust involves three parties: the grantor, the trustee, and the beneficiary.

- The **grantor** (sometimes called the **donor** or **settlor**) is the party who defines the terms (rules) of the trust, transfers property to the trust, and, usually, retains the right to change the trust until his or her death.
- The **trustee** is the party in charge of managing the trust (e.g., making investment decisions, distributing assets to the beneficiary when applicable, and fulfilling any administrative requirements). The trustee owes a fiduciary duty to the beneficiary, and the trustee must manage the trust in such a way that is in keeping with the terms of the trust.
- The **beneficiary** (or beneficiaries) is the party for whose benefit the assets in the trust are held/managed.

These parties may be actual human persons, or they may be legal entities. For instance, you could name a law firm or CPA firm as the trustee to a trust. And it's common to name a non-profit organization as a beneficiary of a trust.

The trust may also designate somebody as a **successor trustee**, to take over when the initial trustee dies, becomes incapacitated, or relinquishes the role.

The trust may also designate one or more parties as **secondary beneficiaries** (also referred to as **contingent beneficiaries**), for whose benefit the assets would be managed if the primary beneficiary has died.

Another important point is that, while there are three parties to a trust, one person may actually be in multiple roles—or even all three roles.

More Trust Terminology

A trust can be an inter vivos trust or a testamentary trust. An **inter vivos trust** is created by the grantor during his or her lifetime, whereas a **testamentary trust** is created at the time of the grantor's death. That is, with a testamentary trust, the grantor's will provides for the trust to be created and funded upon his or her death. (If you are the PR of your spouse's estate, and his/her will includes terms for a testamentary trust, it will be your responsibility to distribute the appropriate assets from the estate to the trust in order to fund the trust in keeping with the will's provisions.)

A trust can be revocable or irrevocable. With a **revocable trust**, the grantor can change the terms of the trust (or even terminate it completely) as long as he/she is still alive and of sound mind. With an **irrevocable trust**, there are some exceptions, but changes generally cannot be made once the trust has been created.

EXAMPLE: Collin is the grantor of a trust (i.e., he funded it with his own assets). The trust is set up so that Collin is also the trustee and beneficiary while he is still alive, with his sister named as the successor trustee and his children named as the secondary beneficiaries.

One way to think about this is that before Collin created the trust, he had various rights in his assets. When he created and funded the trust, he transferred some of the rights in his assets to himself as the grantor, some to himself as trustee, and some to himself as beneficiary. Consequently, he retained all the rights in his assets that he held before the trust was created, but he now holds them in different capacities. In so doing, he creates a mechanism for others to act in the various capacities in the future.

As time passes, his sister may take over management of the trust as successor trustee when, for example, Collin becomes unable to manage his assets on his own. In addition, at Collin's death, if his sister hadn't already, she would become successor trustee and his children, the contingent beneficiaries, would become entitled to the benefits of the trust.

Note that there is no successor grantor because the main power given to the grantor is to change the trust. However, when the grantor dies, a trust becomes irrevocable, and cannot be changed.

More Trust Usage Examples

With the above terminology discussion out of the way, we can go through a few examples of cases in which a trust would be useful.

EXAMPLE: Susie is a widow with three adult children (two daughters and a son). Her son has a long history of making poor financial decisions. In Susie's will, rather than leaving 1/3 of her assets to each of her children outright, she leaves 1/3 to each of the daughters, and she leaves the remaining 1/3 to a trust. Susie names her son as the beneficiary of the trust, and she names her attorney as the trustee. This way her son still receives the benefits of the assets, but somebody else (the trustee) will be making the decisions as to how to invest and spend the assets.

EXAMPLE: Luther and Harriette are married, in their 60s. Harriette has two adult children from a prior marriage. Luther does not get along with Harriette's children. Harriette is concerned that if she dies before Luther and her assets are simply left to Luther at her death, he will ultimately disinherit her children. As a result, Harriette provides in her will for a testamentary trust to be created upon her death and for her assets to be placed into that trust. The terms of the trust are that Luther will receive the income from the assets while he is alive, and then the assets will be left to her children upon Luther's death.

EXAMPLE: Nigel and Veronica have an adult son who is disabled. The son is currently receiving Social Security disability benefits. And because of his low level of income and assets, he also qualifies for Supplemental Security Income (SSI) and Medicaid. If they simply leave their assets to him outright, he would lose eligibility for SSI and Medicaid. Instead, they create a special needs trust, which will receive their assets upon the death of the second spouse. Their son is named as beneficiary of the trust, and a trusted CPA is named as the trustee. Because the son has no control over the assets in the trust, it will not disqualify him from receiving SSI or Medicaid. The trustee will not be allowed to outright give the assets to the son, but the assets can be used for a variety of purposes for the benefit of the son.

Trusts are sometimes created with a goal of reducing potential estate tax costs. One of the ways to do this is to transfer assets to an irrevocable trust (thereby removing the assets from the grantor's taxable estate), often while maintaining some current benefit (e.g., the right to take income from the assets for a period of years). By transferring assets now, the grantor will often have a taxable gift, but a significant advantage is that the gift is at today's value, rather than at some more highly appreciated value at the date of the grantor's death. There are many different variations on this concept though (e.g., intentionally defective grantor trusts, qualified personal residence trusts, charitable remainder trusts, etc.).

Another common use of trusts is simply to avoid probate. Assets that are placed in a trust do not have to go through probate upon the death of the grantor, because the terms of the trust govern how the assets are transferred, not state probate laws.

Responsibilities as Trustee

If you are the trustee of a trust (e.g., one created by your spouse before his/her death or a testamentary trust created upon your spouse's death) you have certain responsibilities. Your responsibilities and powers as trustee should be spelled out in the trust document.

The role of trustee is akin to the role of personal representative of an estate in that you have a fiduciary duty to the beneficiaries of the trust. You must manage the assets in a prudent way for the benefit of the beneficiaries, and you must put the interests of the beneficiaries above your own interests (other than to the extent that you are a beneficiary).

Also like the role of personal representative, you have the option to decline to serve as trustee.

The details vary by state law, but as trustee you have a duty to keep the beneficiaries informed as to the administration of the trust. This often includes providing (at least) annual statements as to the trust's assets, liabilities, income, expenses, and distributions. If/when the trust is closed, you should send each beneficiary a record of all the major actions you took as trustee, including distributions made.

As with an estate, a trust is a taxable entity.[1] If a trust has gross income of $600 or more for the year (or any taxable income more than zero), the trustee must file a Form 1041 reporting (and potentially paying tax on) that income.

If the trust owns any valuable property that does not have an easily determinable market value (e.g., real estate), it's important to get it appraised.

---

[1] There are some exceptions while the grantor is still alive. That is, with some types of trusts, the trust's income is simply treated as if it were the grantor's income. However, once the grantor dies, the trust will be considered a separate taxpayer going forward.

Beneficiaries need to know the value of the property so that they know their basis in the property. In addition, knowing the value may be important for determining what distributions should be made to whom. (For example, if the terms of the trust state that half of the assets are to be distributed to you as the surviving spouse and the other half are to be distributed to another party—but it does not specify *which* assets go to which party—it's necessary to know the value of all of the assets in order to be able to make appropriate distributions.)

As with everything else you've been doing through this whole process, it's important to keep records of your actions as trustee. Document any significant actions that you take (investment decisions, distributions from the trust, etc.) as well as your reason for those actions.

Your Rights as Beneficiary

If you are the beneficiary of a trust, you have the right to have the assets managed for your benefit (though not for your *exclusive* benefit, unless you are the sole beneficiary).

As a beneficiary you also have a right to regular communication from the trustee. As described above, the trustee is usually required to provide annual statements as to the finances of the trust. You also (probably) have a right to have the terms of the trust provided to you, upon request.

If you feel that the trustee is not satisfying his or her duties, you can ask a court to remove that trustee. If the court agrees, the next person named in the trust document would become the trustee. (If no such successor trustee is named in the trust document, the court may appoint one.)

Simple Summary

- A trust is a legal entity that can own property. There are many types of trusts, each with a different purpose, but the most common uses of trusts are to avoid probate, minimize estate taxes, or exert some control over a pool of assets after the grantor dies or becomes incapacitated.

- The grantor/donor is the party who creates the trust, defines its terms, and funds the trust with assets. The trustee is the party in charge of managing the trust. And the beneficiary is the party for whom the trust's assets are managed.

- Assets owned by a trust do not have to pass through probate upon the death of the grantor.

- If you are the trustee of a trust, you have a fiduciary duty to the trust's beneficiaries.

- If you are the beneficiary of a trust, you have the right to have the assets managed for your benefit, the right to communication from the trustee, and the right to petition a court for a replacement trustee if you feel that the trustee is not satisfying his/her duties.

Acknowledgements

My sincere gratitude goes to three attorneys who generously contributed their time and expertise: Lee Aronson of Shreveport, Louisiana; Randi Grassgreen of Boulder, Colorado; and Matthew Sullivan of Waltham, Massachusetts.

Bogleheads forum members "LadyGeek" and "dodecahedron" also very kindly gave their time and shared their knowledge and experiences as surviving spouses. Thank you both! This book is much better as a result of your contributions.

And to Kalinda (my spouse) and Debbi (my mom), thank you. For everything—including reading yet another book.

Also by Mike Piper

Can I Retire? How to Manage Your Retirement Savings, Explained in 100 Pages or Less

Investing Made Simple: Investing in Index Funds Explained in 100 Pages or Less

Taxes Made Simple: Income Taxes Explained in 100 Pages or Less

Social Security Made Simple: Social Security Retirement Benefits Explained in 100 Pages or Less

Independent Contractor, Sole Proprietor, and LLC Taxes Explained in 100 Pages or Less

LLC vs. S-Corp vs. C-Corp Explained in 100 Pages or Less

Accounting Made Simple: Accounting Explained in 100 Pages or Less

Cost Accounting Made Simple: Cost Accounting Explained in 100 Pages or Less

Corporate Finance Made Simple: Corporate Finance Explained in 100 Pages or Less

Microeconomics Made Simple: Basic Microeconomic Principles Explained in 100 Pages or Less

About the Author

Mike is the author of several books as well as the popular blog ObliviousInvestor.com. He is a Missouri licensed CPA. Mike's writing has been featured in many places, including *The Wall Street Journal, Money, Forbes*, and *MarketWatch*. Mike is also the creator of the Open Social Security calculator, which has been featured in *The New York Times, The Wall Street Journal*, and elsewhere.

INDEX